WHO IS GOD?

Bringing the Infinite into Focus

J. VERNON MCGEE

THOMAS NELSON PUBLISHERS®

Nashville

Published in Nashville, Tennessee, by Thomas Nelson, Inc.

Library of Congress Cataloging–in–Publication Data

McGee, J. Vernon (John Vernon), 1904–
    Who is God? : bringing the infinite into focus / J. Vernon McGee.
        p. cm.
    Includes bibliographical references.
    ISBN 0-7852-6934-7
    1. God. I. Title.
BT102.M4253   1999
231—dc21

99–37463
CIP

Printed in the United States of America
1 2 3 4 5 6 7 BVG 04 03 02 01 00 99

CONTENTS

INTRODUCTION

A skeptic once remarked that most Christians do not have a speaking acquaintanceship with God and would not recognize Him if they met Him face-to-face on the street. Even Dr. McGee noted that there is an appalling ignorance of God among Christians.

Let us address this accusation with an illustration: How would you respond if you were asked to describe your closest friend? Maybe you'd begin by remarking on how tall he is and point out the color of his hair and eyes. Or perhaps you'd mention his generosity and sense of humor. Regardless of what traits come to mind, the point is that you know your close friends well and could think of a great deal to say about their appearance, their likes and dislikes, and the little idiosyncrasies that make them unique personalities.

Imagine then what you would say in answer to the question: Who is God? Could you describe what He looks like, how He feels after a tragedy or a triumph, what He is doing in your life and in this world today? Or would you be hard-pressed for a clear and precise answer? In attempting to know God we are posed with a problem. Why? Because God is Spirit, He is the "High and Lofty One" seated in the heavens. It is true that two thousand years ago He took human form in the person of His Son and walked here among us, but essentially God is Spirit.

Scripture, however, states unequivocally that it is possible to know God intimately. God took the initiative, and we can know what He has chosen to reveal to us regarding Himself. Although nature gives us precious little direct information about Him, we can come to know Him through the Lord Jesus Christ and through a careful study of His Word.

There are two things to keep in mind as we begin this grand endeavor of getting to know God better. The first is that our God is infinite. There are absolutely no limits to Him, nor is there anything found in creation to which we can compare Him. The second is that we are finite creatures. Therefore, it is impossible for us ever to comprehend fully the infinite depth, height, and breadth of who God is.

The messages contained here do not attempt to compartmentalize or condense God. They merely bring certain aspects of our infinite God into focus so that in our limited human understanding we might better comprehend His supreme greatness, His extreme holiness, His boundless capacity for love, and His provision of a way to draw us close to Himself.

Thru The Bible Radio, 1999

CHAPTER 1

WHERE IS GOD AND WHAT DOES HE DO?

In studying who God is, we are often in the realm of the abstract and the obtuse. We talk about His absolute attributes, and they are indeed extraordinary. We talk about His character, what He is innately, and the contemplation of that is staggering indeed. When dwelling on these aspects of God, human comparisons are impossible. The issues of where God is and what He does, on the other hand, are more tangible and substantial. They take us out of the imponderables and down to earth where we can deal with that which is relevant and germane.

What we are attempting to do in this study is to bring God into focus so that we might know Him a little better. But right at the very outset may I make a distinction and utter a word of caution. We're not now discussing God as Creator. We are not going back to the verse, "In the beginning God created the heavens and the earth" (Genesis 1:1). What we're talking about here is something altogether different: God's present relationship to His universe, that which He exercises at this very moment.

The average church member does not have a solid understanding of God's relationship to His creation. A great many people would like to point to the sky and say, "God is up there." When we fully comprehend this subject I trust we will never again make the mistake of pointing up and saying, "God is in that direction." The reason is because God *touches* His creation. He rubs shoulders with His universe. And that's where "the heavens declare the glory of God; and the firmament shows His handiwork" (Psalm 19:1).

Creation for most people is the most convincing proof of the existence of God. Through the years, pollsters have found that a surprisingly large number of people in America believe in the existence of God. Then a second question is asked, "What proof do you offer for the existence of God?" The reason given that stands out above all others—in fact, twice as much as any other—is the order and majesty of the world around us. So you can see that folk today do turn to this universe as the basis of proof for the existence of God. It has always been that way. Thomas Aquinas, who presented four great reasons for the existence of God, used as his fourth reason: "The scale of perfection evident in the universe implies the existence of an absolute standard, a perfect being." And that argument is scriptural because, you will recall, it was the apostle Paul in the Book of Romans who said,

> **Because what may be known of God is manifest in them, for God has shown it to them. For since the creation of the world His invisible attributes are clearly seen, being understood by the things that are made, even His eternal power and Godhead, so that they are without excuse.** (1:19–20)

A poet put it this way:

> The world is a bud from the bower of His beauty;
> The sun is a spark from the light of His wisdom;
> The sky is a bubble on the sea of His power.

So creation today does have a message for man, and it speaks of the existence of God and His tremendous power. Wherever you look in history you will find that mankind has believed in the existence of God, and the basis for that belief has always been the creation. This is understandable considering that God is involved in an active relationship with His creation. There are three words that describe and define God's relation to His universe. Now these three words are awe-inspiring and formidable. We need to understand them, because they are scriptural words: God is *omnipresent*, God is *omnipotent*, and God is *omniscient*.

God Is Omnipresent

What do we mean when we say that God is omnipresent? We mean simply this: He is present everywhere in His creation, in this universe that He has made. He is present with you at this very moment, but that does not exclude His being in China or Berlin at the same time. God today is present *everywhere* in His universe. You can't exclude Him. One morning at the breakfast table an atheist said, "God is nowhere." His daughter who was a Christian said, "You are right. God is now here." They are the same letters of the alphabet but have a very different meaning. But God *is* now here—that is the language of Scripture as we read in Psalm 139:

> **If I ascend into heaven, You are there; if I make my bed in hell** [that is, if I make my bed where the dead are]**, behold, You are there. If I take the wings of the morning, and dwell in the uttermost parts of the sea, even there Your hand shall lead me, and Your right hand shall hold me.** (vv. 8–10)

David is saying that the omnipresence of God is absolutely overwhelming. He could not get away from God. In fact, God could track him better than a bloodhound and follow him better than the FBI. It didn't make any difference where David was, because God was there waiting for him. When David told Him good-bye at this station, God was the first one to greet him at the next station. God is everywhere. The same concept was shared with Jeremiah:

**"Am I a God near at hand," says the LORD,
"And not a God afar off?"** (Jeremiah 23:23)

In other words, "I'm a God right here but also I am a God afar off. I have not forgotten the heathen—I'm out yonder in other places also." And again He says, "Do I not fill heaven and earth?" (Jeremiah 23:24). And He certainly does, my beloved. The interesting thing that always puzzles me is this: All of God is here, and all of God is in China. God is everywhere, all of Him, at the same time. We today are not in the foot of God, we are not in the arm of God, but as Paul said to the Athenians,

So that they should seek the Lord, in the hope that they might grope for Him and find Him, though He is not far from each one of us; for in Him we live and move and have our being . . . . (Acts 17:27–28)

So at this moment all of God is present, and you can never go anyplace where you're out of the presence of God—for *all* of God is present *everywhere*.

Now for God to be everywhere He must be pretty big, so let's take a telescope and look at the size of God. The universe that we live in is a sizable one. Since the time when scientists first started probing outer space, they have found that the universe is at least eight times larger than they thought. Our solar system is just one of many that make up our galactic system. They've now discovered one hundred million galactic systems, and in each one it is estimated that there are two hundred billion stars! Now when you multiply one hundred million by two hundred billion you get a figure that I can't even deal with. I don't know what it is, but to us it means that there are a whole lot of stars!

May I say to you, that unimaginable expanse of stars and systems is *God's* creation. And He's yonder this morning at the very end of His universe as well as being present here this moment. Move out into the realm of the stars and think about God being everywhere in this vast universe. God is not only *in* creation; He is greater than creation. He's not a prisoner in this universe; God *encompasses* His universe!

That's not all. Let's put down the telescope (it makes me dizzy), and let's take up the microscope for a moment. We want to look at the lowly atom.

As far as I know they don't yet have a microscope that will allow us to see the atom—it's too small. But I assure you that all of God is in every one of those atoms. Man was rather convinced of that many years ago in Hiroshima. Oh, the tremendous power of God in the little atom! So you see, God is present in His creation, but He also transcends His creation!

I heard a lecture at Vanderbilt University years ago. I wish I had known then what I know now because the man who spoke said, "We know that the ancient Hebrews had a very limited idea of God. They thought they could build a house and God could move into it." The trouble with that brother was that he knew a great deal of philosophy but he was practically ignorant of the Bible. I'm amazed that he was not acquainted with 1 Kings 8:27 when he made that statement. But I can't find fault with him, because I didn't know it then either. Actually, when Solomon dedicated the temple, this is what he said,

But will God indeed dwell on the earth? Behold, heaven and the heaven of heavens cannot contain You. How much less this temple which I have built! (1 Kings 8:27)

They understood in the Old Testament that God couldn't move into a house. Israel understood that the heaven of heavens could not contain God.

It was Isaiah who called Him "the High and Lofty One who inhabits eternity" (Isaiah 57:15). They had a tremendously exalted conception of God, if you please. But may I say that they also knew He was in their midst. Just because He's inhabiting eternity doesn't mean He is not close by. Remember that in Jeremiah 23:23 He asked, "Am I a God near at hand . . . and not a God afar off?" He is very close at hand. The Lord Jesus said,

> **For where two or three are gathered together in My name, I am there in the midst of them.** (Matthew 18:20)

Today when two or three humble believers come together, the God of eternity is present. That is mind-boggling. He is present here this day. That is a thought that should overwhelm all of us!

Pagan philosophies have wrestled with this problem of knowing where God is, and they've come up with two extreme viewpoints. One is the philosophy known as pantheism, and it is pagan to the very core. It asserts that God is equal to His creation, that in a sense all of creation is God. We see it in Buddhism; Plato adopted it; and we find it in old theological liberalism. This is the reason some of the old liberals claimed that Jesus was divine. Someone asked Dr. Fosdick, a prominent liberal years ago, if he thought Jesus was divine. His reply was, "Yes, but aren't we all?" In other words, God is the sum total of His universe. You just add up everything in the universe, and the total is God. Then there was another extreme developed by the German philosopher Kant. He said that God is transcendent; that is to say, He is not an active participant in this universe. That group's thought was that God wound up this universe as you would a watch, and then He went off and left it.

May I say to you that the Word of God is very careful to guard against these two extreme viewpoints. Listen to what the Scriptures have to say. The apostle Paul stated it well:

> **One God and Father of all, who is above all, and through all, and in you all.**
> (Ephesians 4:6)

At this moment God is above all, but He is also throughout His universe, and He also dwells in the heart of every humble sinner who comes to Christ and trusts Him as Savior.

We are also told in Scripture that heaven is the home of God. The psalmist said,

> **Unto You I lift up my eyes, O You who dwell in the heavens.** (Psalm 123:1)

We need today that exalted viewpoint of God, the viewpoint that Isaiah had when he went into the temple and saw there the One "high and lifted up." Oh, how America needs that conception of Almighty God today! But the very moment we speak of Him being in heaven, we must also add that God accommodated Himself for His people. When they were journeying through the wilderness He took up His dwelling place among them in the tabernacle, and they met God there. Every Israelite knew that the place to worship God was at the tabernacle and that you couldn't honestly worship Him out on the golf course or down at the beach. The way to approach God in those days was through the tabernacle. And when David wanted to build a temple, God reminded him, "I took up My place in a tent. I have never asked for a permanent dwelling place for the very simple reason I wanted to be unto My people what they were. When they were pilgrims and strangers I wanted to go along with them." (see 1 Chronicles 17 and 2 Samuel 7). Friend, that's the reason we can't build a house and say that God dwells in it. He is with His people today. He *indwells* every believer in the person of the Holy Spirit. Actually we are told that the believers are the temple of God today by the presence of the Holy Spirit within them.

When we come to the New Testament we find again that God is localized. Let me paraphrase John 1:14 a little: "The Word was made flesh and pitched His tent among us." The greatest miracle in this world was the incarnation of Jesus

Christ—God, the One who created this universe, the One who was at the very beginning.

In the beginning was the Word, and the Word was with God, and the Word was God. He was in the beginning with God. All things were made through Him, and without Him nothing was made that was made ... And the Word became flesh and dwelt [pitched His tent] among us, and we beheld His glory, the glory as of the only begotten of the Father, full of grace and truth. (John 1:1–3, 14)

If you're going to know God you will have to come to Jesus Christ. My beloved, at this moment He is closer to you than the one sitting next to you. He is closer than your hands and your feet. He said to those who are His own, "Lo, I am with you always, even to the end of the age" (Matthew 28:20). And one of the loveliest things He ever said about God was this:

Are not two sparrows sold for a copper coin? And not one of them falls to the ground apart from your Father's will. (Matthew 10:29)

That's how our translation reads, but that's not what He really said. Literally, He said that every sparrow falls in the presence of God. That's wonderful! While out dove hunting one day in Texas, I was watching a dove up in a tree. Being Scottish and economical, I was waiting for two doves so I could get both of them with one shot. As I was waiting, all of a sudden that dove just toppled over. I wondered who shot it, but nobody shot it. That dove just dropped dead. May I say to you, God was present there. The most wonderful thing in the world is that God, in a sense, goes to the funeral of every sparrow, every bird! Those little chirping birds all around us—nobody pays any attention to them. But every time one of them falls, God is right there. I don't know about you, but that's rather overwhelming to me! Our God is omnipresent—present everywhere.

God Is Omnipotent

Our God is omnipotent. That means that He is all-powerful and can do all things that are the object of power. There is, however, a self-limitation in God. *God can do all He wills to do, but He doesn't will to do all He can do.* In other words, He limits Himself. Here are some ridiculous examples: Can God make an old man in a minute? Could He make a world where two plus two equals five? Can God sin? Can God die? Can God make a mountain that has no valleys around it? Can God make round squares? And can He make snarks and bojums and abracadabras? Can God do these things? I say to you, God can do *anything* that's the object of power, but He doesn't do all He *can* do because He doesn't *will* to do it. An example of that is sin. God does not sin because He wills not to sin. To me that's the same as saying that He cannot sin. Why? Because of His nature and His character, it is His own limitation that He has put upon Himself.

God is present everywhere, and He possesses all power. Have you ever gone through the New Testament and noticed the Scriptures where it says, "He is able"? Let me give just three:

Therefore He is also able to save to the uttermost those who come to God through Him, since He ever lives to make intercession for them. (Hebrews 7:25)

God loves us and He is able to save us, but not because of His great love. In the beautiful story of Boaz and Ruth, the reason Boaz could act as Ruth's kinsman redeemer was because he was able to pay the price of her redemption. His love for her gave the motivation. In the same way, Jesus Christ was able to pay the price for our redemption. In so doing, He became our Kinsman Redeemer. Salvation is essentially a love story, but love without power is helpless. We have an illustration of that at the tomb of Lazarus where love weeps. But power says, "Lazarus, come forth!" We have a God who is able.

And then,

Who are you to judge another's servant? To his own master he stands or falls. Indeed, he will be made to stand, for God is able to make him stand. (Romans 14:4)

Is there a Christian whom you've been criticizing and finding fault with? Well, God is able to make that person stand.

Finally we have,

And God is able to make all grace abound toward you, that you, always having all sufficiency in all things, may have an abundance for every good work. (2 Corinthians 9:8)

"God is able to make all grace abound toward you." He is able to supply you with all the grace it will take to get you to heaven. No one can cut off His supply.

God Is Omniscient

God knows all things, He is omniscient. When preparing to discuss a subject like this, a seminary professor of mine would say, "If you have brains prepare to use them now," because we're moving into "heavy stuff"—the omniscience of God.

First of all, He has foreknowledge. Now, follow me very carefully. I don't want to be tedious, but I want to keep you alert and thinking with me. This is very important. God has foreknowledge— He knows the outcome of the plan He's working on for the universe today. He has perfect knowledge, so there will be no fortuitous concurrence of circumstances as far as He's concerned. There will be no contingencies at all. I remember a Japanese proverb that says, "God has forgotten to forget." In other words, God knows it all, my beloved. Listen to the confirmation of Scripture:

And there is no creature hidden from His sight, but all things are naked and open to the eyes of Him to whom we must give account. (Hebrews 4:13)

God knows everything about His universe, down to the most minute detail: "He counts the number of the stars; He calls them all by name" (Psalm 147:4). We are told that even the hairs of our head are numbered (Matthew 10:30). Your mother never did *that* for you! When you run your fingers through your hair and one strand falls out, God knows about it and subtracts one from the total. No wonder David cried out, "Such knowledge is too wonderful for me!" (Psalm 139:6). And, friends, it is too wonderful for any of us to comprehend.

Oh, the depth of the riches both of the wisdom and knowledge of God! How unsearchable are His judgments and His ways past finding out! (Romans 11:33)

How wonderful He is!

Therefore, in this plan that God is working on He is not sitting on the edge of His throne biting His fingernails, wondering what to do next. There is no crisis in heaven. God today is leading the parade of His creation, and it never turns a corner until He turns the corner first. He is in charge of this universe. God is in the saddle today. He doesn't play the stock market; He *runs* the stock market. He doesn't wonder who the winners will be; He is the One who decides who will be the champion.

The Greeks had a proverb: "The dice of the gods are loaded." God says to you, my beloved, "Don't roll the dice with Me because I always know what's coming up. Bet against Me and you will lose." My friend, don't think you can play with God. Don't think you can live fast and loose and get by with it with Him.

Do not be deceived, God is not mocked; for whatever a man sows, that he will also reap. (Galatians 6:7)

Why? Because God has determined it that way, and if you don't like it, it's too bad for you. God has no notion of changing His mind because you do not approve of what He is doing. He will go through with His program.

The psalmist said,

You have set our iniquities before You, Our secret sins in the light of Your countenance. (Psalm 90:8)

Dr. Lewis Sperry Chafer, founder of Dallas Theological Seminary, used to put it like this: "What is secret sin down here is open scandal in heaven." What you think you're getting by with is disgusting to the angels, and they know all about it. We are well-known to God today. He knows every thought and every word that is on your tongue— even the ones you started to say but refrained from speaking out loud.

As far as He is concerned He does not have to memorize; He never ties a string around His finger to remind Himself of something. God today has no regrets of the past, He has no problems of the present, He has no forebodings about the future. He knows the direction He's going. He is the Architect of this universe, and He has the blueprints in His hands. They're being followed to the exact line and detail. That's the foreknowledge of God.

Let's move on to something that's vastly more important and greater than that: the self-knowledge of God. Do you know that this covers a great deal? God knows Himself, and that's quite an education. There are no limits to who He is—God is infinite. Therefore, He has infinite knowledge. The difficulty with you and me is that we do not know ourselves. Socrates developed a philosophy derived from this concept: "Know thyself." Get acquainted with yourself. The trouble with most of us is that we are like Simon Peter. The reason Simon Peter said, "I'll not deny You, I'll stick right by You," was that he didn't know Simon Peter. You and I do not know ourselves. But God knows Himself perfectly, and I believe that He is going to be one of the subjects we will study in eternity. To spend eternity just coming to know God is going to be a very worthwhile pursuit. It's going to cause us to go down on our faces repeatedly as we realize how wonderful God is. If right now we could comprehend just how wonderful God really is, we would be shouting hallelujahs. But we do not know Him very well today.

God, being omniscient, also knows all that is knowable. A preacher was introducing a visiting brother one day in his pulpit. He was using grand, eloquent terms and he said, "We have with us today a brother who knows the unknowable. He can do the undoable and he can unscrew the unscrewable." May I say to you that God is the

One who *fulfills* that. God knows the unknowable. God knows everything that's actual and possible. He not only knows the plan He's working on today, but when He started out there was an infinite number of plans with all sorts of ramifications and details, and He chose this plan because it's the best plan. What right have you and I to question God today? He's working on that which is the very best plan. How wonderful, how glorious it is! He knows the end from the beginning, and He chose this plan because it was the best one; that's what omniscience means.

In our attempt to bring God into focus, consider this very carefully: *You* were in the plan of God. The very fact that you are in existence today means that in eternity past you were in the mind of God. David, that sweet singer of Israel, wrote:

> **For You have formed my inward parts; You have covered me in my mother's womb. I will praise You, for I am fearfully and wonderfully made; marvelous are Your works, and that my soul knows very well. My frame was not hidden from You, when I was made in secret, and skillfully wrought in the lowest parts of the earth. Your eyes saw my substance, being yet unformed. And in Your book they all were written, the days fashioned for me, when as yet there were none of them.** (Psalm 139:13–16)

Such knowledge is too wonderful for me! The One who counts the hairs on your head, the One who knows you as no one else, can say this to you: "Just as He chose us in Him before the foundation of the world, that we should be holy and without blame before Him in love" (Ephesians 1:4). You say, "Preacher, how do you know that?" I know it because our Lord said,

> **Most assuredly, I say to you, he who hears My word and believes in Him who sent Me has everlasting life, and shall not come into judgment, but has passed from death into life.** (John 5:24)

In "he who hears My word," *he* is generic, meaning any human being. Well, you're a human being. "He who hears My word"—you are hearing it right now. After reading this passage you cannot say that you never heard it. You did! "He who hears My word and believes in Him who sent Me"—now that's where you come in. He has provided an opportunity for you to believe. It's up to you; the responsibility is yours.

> **Ho! Everyone who thirsts, come to the waters.** (Isaiah 55:1)

Everyone? Yes, everyone. But wait just a minute—there is a limitation. You must thirst.

Are you thirsty? Do you want what God has to offer you? You can walk away and say, "I'll have none of that!" Friend, that's up to you, it is your business. But you won't fool God. He has made a way for you. The Son of God says,

> **Behold, I stand at the door and knock. If anyone hears My voice and opens the door, I will come in to him and dine with him, and he with Me.** (Revelation 3:20)

Anyone—that's you. You can open the door, but you yourself have to do it. Or you can leave the door shut. You can even slam it in His face. He lets you do that now, but someday the opportunity to turn to the Savior will end.

On the Day of Pentecost, Peter turned to the crowd and said,

> **Him, being delivered by the determined counsel and foreknowledge of God, you have taken by lawless hands, have crucified, and put to death.** (Acts 2:23)

In other words, "Your hands are red, you're guilty. But you didn't fool God. He permitted His Son to die in order that you, guilty as you are, could be saved." Three thousand were saved there that day. Out of that crowd there were men who probably had ridiculed Him and actually spit on

Him—the God of this universe. Yet He saved them!

I close with this:

> The Maker of the universe, as man for man
>   was made a curse.
> The claims of law which He had made, unto the
>   uttermost He paid.
> His holy fingers made the bough which grew
>   the thorns that crowned His brow.
> The nails that pierced His hands were mined
>   in secret places He designed.
> He made the forest whence there sprung the
>   tree on which His body hung.
> He died upon a cross of wood, yet made the hill
>   on which it stood.
> The sky that darkened o'er His head, by Him
>   above the earth was spread.
> The sun that hid Him from God's face, by His
>   decree was poised in space.
> The spear which spilled His precious blood was
>   tempered in the fires of God.
> The grave in which His form was laid was
>   hewn in rocks His hands had made.
> The throne on which He now appears was His
>   from everlasting years.
> But a new glory crowns His brow, and every
>   knee to Him shall bow.
>
> (Author unknown)

He is the Creator of this universe. He has it in perfect control today. You and I are just little creatures, but He loves us enough to die for us. And when you reject Him you have committed the sin that makes murder and stealing and lying and adultery look white in comparison; you have turned your back on the Son of God.

CHAPTER 2

HOW BIG IS GOD?

"How big is God?" is a pertinent question, especially in this age of space exploration and expanding technology. A writer once put it like this:

> Is the Christ of the Gospels, imagined and loved within the dimensions of a Mediterranean world, capable of still embracing and still forming the center of our prodigiously expanded universe? Is the world not in the process of becoming more vast, more close, more dazzling than Jehovah? Will it not burst our religion asunder, eclipse our God?

I think if you study the Scriptures, you will find that the universe is not becoming too big for God.

This is also a question that might come into the mind of a child, but that a wise man cannot answer thoroughly and to the satisfaction of all. It's like the old chestnut—"Can God make a rock so big that even He cannot lift it?" The reason it is so difficult to answer is that we have no yardstick to put down by the side of God. He is not "so many" feet long; He is not "so many" feet wide; He is not "so many" miles high. Paul recognized this when he prayed that the Ephesians might know the love of Christ:

> **That you, being rooted and grounded in love, may be able to comprehend with all the saints what is the width and length and depth and height—to know the love of Christ which passes knowledge. . . .**
> (Ephesians 3:17–19)

This means that (humanly speaking) you and I cannot even begin to comprehend the love of God. We do not know how high it is; we do not know how wide it is; we do not know how long it is; we do not know how deep it is. What we do know is only what the Holy Spirit is pleased to open our minds and hearts to. Therefore, Paul prayed that the believers in Ephesus might "know the love of Christ which passes knowledge; that you may be filled with all the fullness of God" (Ephesians 3:19).

Not only is it a hard question to answer, but it is an old question, this matter of knowing how big God is. In fact, it's found in what is probably the most ancient book in the Bible—the Book of Job. Zophar raised the question when he asked,

> **Can you search out the deep things of God? Can you find out the limits of the Almighty? They are higher than heaven— what can you do? Deeper than Sheol— what can you know? Their measure is longer than the earth and broader than the sea.** (Job 11:7–9)

Then Elihu, when he entered into the conversation with Job, added:

> **Behold, God is great, and we do not know Him; nor can the number of His years be discovered.** (Job 36:26)

Someone might ask, "How old is God?" But we just can't know these things.

When a person says that the footsteps of God can be found in nature, I say they are not there. The Word of God says they are not there, and the psalmist reminds us of that:

> **Your way was in the sea, Your path in the great waters, and Your footsteps were not known.** (Psalm 77:19)

We can know only two things about God from

nature—His power and His person. The two are
given in Romans 1:20:

> **For since the creation of the world His
> invisible attributes are clearly seen,
> being understood by the things that are
> made, even His eternal power and
> Godhead, so that they are without excuse.**

The psalmist also recorded,

> **Great is the LORD, and greatly to be
> praised; and His greatness is unsearch-
> able.** (Psalm 145:3)

You see, we need to be very reverent and humble
about this subject of God's magnitude; only the
arrogant and the agnostic will speak out about it
in any dogmatic fashion. We can know only what
the Word of God reveals.

According to the Scriptures, God does not fit
the dimensions of this world. He has no reference
at all to distance and time. There is nothing to
which we may compare Him, and He constantly
reminded His people in the Old Testament of that
very fact. Listen to what God said to the nation of
Israel:

> **Now see that I, even I, am He, and there is
> no God besides Me; I kill and I make alive; I**

wound and I heal; nor is there any who can deliver from My hand. (Deuteronomy 32:39)

Isaiah, who was up against a nation enslaved by idolatry and polytheism, spoke for God:

Tell and bring forth your case; yes, let them take counsel together. Who has declared this from ancient time? Who has told it from that time? Have not I, the LORD? And there is no other God besides Me, a just God and a Savior; there is none besides Me. Look to Me, and be saved, all you ends of the earth! For I am God, and there is no other. (Isaiah 45:21–22)

To whom will you liken Me, and make Me equal and compare Me, that we should be alike? (Isaiah 46:5)

Also, Paul spoke along this line:

Therefore concerning the eating of things offered to idols, we know that an idol is nothing in the world, and that there is no other God but one. (1 Corinthians 8:4)

There is not, nor has there ever been, a single thing in creation by which to compare God. He is the only One of His kind.

My friend, let me make this rather startling statement: You have seen something that God has never seen. The fact of the matter is, you see it every day. Do you know what it is? It's your equal—you see your equal every day. God has never seen His equal. We can say, "That's a tall man," or, "That's a short man." And why do we say that? We say it because it's a relative term— we're thinking in terms of other human beings. That is the only way we know that a person is tall or short. But can we say that God is tall or God is short? Of course not, because there is nothing in creation to compare Him to.

The Greeks built a grand civilization that affects the world even today. They were probably the most brilliant people who ever walked this earth. But their conception of God—or in this case, their gods—was stupidly formed on human terms rather than on spiritual terms, because every man without the leading of the Holy Spirit must be spiritually stupid. So what the Greeks ended up with for their deities was a big bunch of overgrown babies on the top of Mount Olympus. Their gods were nothing more than human beings blown up to enormous proportions—oversized bantams with pygmy brains.

Therefore, if you and I are to know how big God is, we cannot use nature or human under-standing as our measuring rod. We must have a different kind of tape measure even to attempt to comprehend His girth. But if we did have a measuring stick big enough or a tape measure long enough, do you really think it could measure God? Of course not! We can't measure God in terms of inches and feet, yards and miles, or even light-years. He can't be weighed in pounds or tons. The entire system of mathematics is inadequate to express anything concerning Him. If you think otherwise, then you know nothing about the enormity of our God.

So, how big is God? Well, let's start with the question of how tall He is. And to measure that I want to give you a new yardstick, a new way of measuring Him: God is *infinite*. Having said that, maybe you think I haven't said very much. But according to the Word of God, He *is* infinite:

Great is our Lord, and mighty in power;
His understanding is infinite. (Psalm 147:5)

In fact, God is infinite in every direction; He transcends all limitations of time and space. He is not a prisoner in His creation at all. If you think He has to rely on transportation to get around you are wrong, and if you think that time is writing furrows upon His brow you're wrong about that as well. Time and space make no impression on Him whatsoever; He is not limited by them as are you and I.

Actually, He uses time and space, as He uses

all of His creation, to accomplish His will. In Genesis the Lord tells how He uses time:

> **Is anything too hard for the LORD? At the appointed time I will return to you, according to the time of life, and Sarah shall have a son.** (Genesis 18:14)

God says, "At the appointed time, I'm coming back to you." Even the coming of the Lord Jesus Christ into the world was timed. God made time His servant and bent it in His hand:

> **But when the fullness of the time had come, God sent forth His Son, born of a woman, born under the law.** (Galatians 4:4)

God pinpointed the appropriate time and sent His Son into the world to save us. You and I are subject to time. It rides on our shoulders, and many of us will not be here in a few years because we are creatures of time. But God is not a creature of time. It is part of His creation, and He controls it.

Space, as far as we know, does not have any limits. God also has no limits, known or unknown. Whatever God does, He does it to an infinite degree, or to use a common colloquialism: Whatever God does, He does it in a big way. When He loves, He loves to an infinite degree. When God brings wisdom to bear, it's infinite wisdom. He is infinite—He is above His creation.

Who is like the LORD our God, who dwells on high, who humbles Himself to behold the things that are in the heavens and in the earth? (Psalm 113:5–6)

Did you know that when God looks in upon His creation He has to humble Himself? It's like going down into a dark and musty old basement: "He raises the poor out of the dust, and lifts the needy out of the ash heap" (Psalm 113:7). Although He may have to go into the basement, He is willing to go there so that He might redeem mankind. May I say to you, God is infinite, and neither time nor space can contain Him.

Because God is infinite, it is impossible for a finite creature to know Him completely. Note Isaiah 40:28:

Have you not known? Have you not heard? The everlasting God, the LORD, the Creator of the ends of the earth, neither faints nor is weary. His understanding is unsearchable.

It's ridiculous for man to try to discover the depths of God. It's like the two blind men who went to a circus and came to where the elephants were. One blind man reached out and felt an elephant's side and said, "He's big and flat like a wall." The other blind man took hold of his tail and said, "You're wrong—he's long and thin like a rope." I say to you, any individual today, in attempting to measure God, is like a blind man fooling around with an elephant!

All of creation is inadequate to reveal God to us. This is the reason why, although many scientists study matter and material, they don't know God Himself. The pagan and heathen world, living in darkness and in spiritual blindness, cannot know God. Even the most brilliant scholar in the world cannot know God by only studying the universe. Someone said concerning the late Luther Burbank, the horticulturist who introduced and developed many new breeds of fruits and plants, that he knew thoroughly the garden, but he never did meet the Gardener. And that is the problem with a great many folk who know remarkable and thrilling things about the "garden" but don't know the "Gardener."

Let me illustrate: I drove a Ford car for years, but I never did know Henry Ford. I have seen pictures of him and believe today, if you would show me a picture, I'd know whether it's Henry Ford or not. But I never *knew* him. However, I know something about that Model-T and all of its peculiarities. My, it was an automobile unlike the ones of today! When something goes wrong with my car now I'm helpless, but back in those days all one needed to fix the Model-T was a piece of baling wire and a pair of pliers. It might break down, but almost anybody could fix it. However, my knowledge of the Model-T never did tell me much about Henry Ford himself.

Likewise, you can't define God by His creation. Oh, there have been attempts to do so. When the great assembly of ministers met to form the Westminster Confession of Faith, that was the biggest problem confronting them. Although they had the rest of their catechism written, when they came to the end of their meetings, they had no answer for who God is. They called on a young Scottish preacher by the name of Dr. Gillespie to lead in prayer. He got to his feet and began to pray, "God, Thou who art a Spirit, infinite, eternal and unchangeable in Thy being, wisdom, power, holiness, justice, goodness and truth. . . ." And the whole assembly realized that this was the answer they were looking for. So that's the best they could do, and I think the Westminster Confession of Faith has the finest expression of who God is: "God is a Spirit, infinite, eternal and unchangeable in His being, wisdom, power, holiness, justice, goodness and truth." Does that tell you anything? Well, it doesn't say much, but I don't think you can improve on it for the simple reason that God is not definitive. His attributes are noncommunicable, and many of them we know nothing about.

My beloved, the only way in the world that you and I can know about God is for Him to reveal Himself. Just before our Lord Jesus gave the invitation to men who labor to come unto Him, He said:

> **All things have been delivered to Me by My Father, and no one knows the Son except the Father. Nor does anyone know the Father except the Son, and to whom the Son wills to reveal Him.** (Matthew 11:27)

Apart from Jesus Christ, the only thing you and I can know about God is that He exists and is powerful. That's the reason our Savior came two thousand years ago—not primarily to redeem man, but He came first to reveal God. He spent only six hours on a cross to redeem the world; He spent thirty-three years revealing who God is. And if you are to know God, you will have to go to the Lord Jesus Christ today. You see, God never had a Columbus—nobody ever discovered God. God is *revealed*. You have to come to His revelation and let Him speak to you there, and He speaks only through the Son, the Lord Jesus Christ!

I've said God is infinite. Now, let's go back to a question we started with: Can God make a rock so big He can't lift it? As I mentioned before, God limits Himself; His is a self-limitation, and it is a sign of strength and not weakness. The Lord Jesus could have made the stones into bread. He did not. If I could make stones into bread, I'd put the bakeries out of business. But I can't do that, and you can't do that either. But He could do it! God limits Himself in everything that He does—He's true to His character. If you think He's going around trying to make rocks so big He can't lift them up, then you're on the wrong track. He never does anything absurd or ridiculous. And He will not do anything wrong, which is the same to me as saying He *cannot* do wrong, because He *will* not. The reason He will not do wrong is that He's true to His character. Only God can make a stone so big that He cannot lift it, but He's not in that business today. He's in the business of lifting up men and women whom no one else can lift.

Do we want to know how big He is? Well then, we'll have to ask another question: How much does God weigh? Answering that requires another way of measuring Him, and here it is: God is self-existent. The self-existence of God is one of the most amazing things—it's called the *aseity* of God (I wanted to get that word in for the benefit of the theological students). What it means is that God exists internally, and He does not need any outside help or support to survive. He is entirely self-sufficient.

In Memphis, Tennessee, many years ago there was a rector, a dean in an Episcopal church, whom I knew but won't name. This man decided that he would fast and reach the place where he did not need to take in food at all. When he lost consciousness, they took him to the hospital and began feeding him intravenously. They brought him back to consciousness, and since then he's been eating! However, God does not have to eat. He doesn't shop at the supermarket, and He doesn't rely on food or nourishment to keep up His strength. God said to His people, "Even if I were hungry, I wouldn't tell you! I wouldn't be knocking at your door." The reason is because He doesn't get hungry! He doesn't need food, water, or help of any kind to exist.

Years ago I was told about a preacher who was invited to speak in a church in Mississippi, and the pastor prayed for him before he got up to speak. In his Southern dialect he prayed: "Lawd, props this man up on the sides he leans on." Now I think that is one of the most wonderful prayers I have heard. If you can think of anything better than that to pray for, I'd like to know what it is. "Prop us up on the side we lean on." But God doesn't lean on any side. There's no weakness there in any way at all. He's not subject to accidents; He doesn't carry any life or health insurance; He doesn't get sick; He doesn't eat an apple a day to keep the doctor away. He has no burial insurance, and He hasn't reserved a crypt in the local cemetery. He doesn't have to have an oxygen supply, and He doesn't need to wear a space suit. None of those things concern Him one whit, if you please. God looks to no one! His existence is not contingent on any outside aid or support, and, my friend, nothing will ever go wrong as far as He is concerned.

He is self-existent. It is His nature to be! He is the absolute. Nothing *causes* Him to do anything—*He* causes *everything*! He is the source and author of life. May I say to you, every breath that you breathe, He furnishes it to you. Every flower that blooms gets its life from Him. He is the giver of life.

That is the reason it's so ridiculous for little man to live down here without God. And any person who thinks he or she can go to heaven living without God is wrong! God has to judge one like that, for He is God. A poet wrote this years ago:

No time for God; what fools we are to clutter up
    our lives with common things,
And leave without heart's gate the Lord of life
    and life itself.
No time for God is soon to say no time to eat or
    sleep, or love or die.
Take time for God, or you shall dwarf your
    soul.
And when the death angel comes knocking at
    your door,
A poor, misshaped thing you'll be to step into
    eternity.
No time for God? That day when sickness
    comes or trouble finds you out,

And you cry out to God, will He have time for
you?
No time for God? Some day you'll lay aside this
mortal self
And make your way to worlds unknown.
And when you meet Him face to face,
Will He—should He—have time for you?

                              (Author unknown)

He won't then, but He will now. He'll take time for
you now.

The supreme object of everything that exists is
for the glory of God. If I may go back to the catechism again, What is the chief end of man? The
chief end of man is "to glorify God and enjoy Him
forever." Why do you exist? You do not exist for
yourself; you do not exist to satisfy your selfish
needs; you do not exist to accumulate something
in this world. You exist for *God*. He created you
for Himself, and that's the chief end of man. You
and I fail when our life is not lived for Him. Let
me repeat: The supreme object of everything is to
bring glory to God.

God is not self-seeking either. The glory rightly
belongs to Him. He claims it in the interest of
truth. God is not selfish. He is always self-bestow-
ing. Have you ever noticed that everything He
does and every time He gives, He does it lavishly?
When God makes leaves on trees, He doesn't put
two or three up there. He puts a big supply of
them. And I wish He wouldn't put so many leaves

on my avocado trees. Boy, they fall all year long. He's got plenty of leaves! When God makes grass, He doesn't make just enough to cover your lawn out front. When there is more rain than usual throughout the year, a green carpet covers the entire state of Texas! It doesn't happen very often, but when it does it's a whole lot of grass. May I say to you, when God makes grass, He does it in a big way. And when God makes rocks . . . have you ever driven through Arizona? Does God have rocks! He didn't make only two or three rocks in Arizona— He distributed them lavishly far and wide. On our way to Honolulu we were once told that we were crossing the deepest place in the ocean. Well, I don't know about vertical depth, but God had plenty of water that I could see just looking out horizontally. When He made an ocean, He made plenty of it. Friends, anywhere that you look, He has plenty. When He made stars—oh, He went into the star-making business! You see, anything God does, He does in a big way. He gives lavishly.

My friend,

For God so loved the world that He gave His only begotten Son, that whoever believes in Him should not perish but have everlasting life. (John 3:16)

Do you know the reason that He gave His Son? It's not because He's big and we're little; it's not that He just wanted to be bighearted. The reason

He gave His Son is because you and I are sinners.
There's a poem that says it better than I could:

It's not because God is great and I'm small;
It's not because He lives forever
And my life is but a handbreadth;
It's not because of the difference
Between His omniscience and my ignorance,
His strength and my weakness,
That I'm parted from Him.
Your sins have separated
Between you and your God.
No man, build he Babels ever so high,
Can reach thither.
There's one means by which
The separation is at an end,
By which all objective hindrances to union
And all subjective hindrances
Are alike swept away.
Christ has come, and in Him
The heavens have bended down to touch
And, touching, to bless this low earth,
And man and God are at one once more.

(Author unknown)

God gave His Son because He loves us in a big way.

To conclude, I'll recount the story found in
Philippians, quoting from the Amplified Bible to
bring out something important. Follow very carefully:

Let this same attitude and purpose and [humble] mind be in you which was in Christ Jesus: [Let Him be your example in humility:] Who, although being essentially one with God and in the form of God [possessing the fullness of the attributes which make God God], did not think this equality with God was a thing to be eagerly grasped or retained, but stripped Himself [of all privileges and rightful dignity], so as to assume the guise of a servant (slave), in that He became like men and was born a human being. And after He had appeared in human form, He abased and humbled Himself [still further] and carried His obedience to the extreme of death, even the death of the cross! (Philippians 2:5–8 AMPLIFIED)

When Christ came down to this earth, He emptied Himself—emptied Himself of what? There are some who say He emptied Himself of His Deity. He did not! He said, "He who has seen Me has seen the Father" (John 14:9). He is God—not 99.44 percent God, but 100 percent God. "I and My Father are one" (John 10:30). Jesus *is* God. But it says that He stripped or emptied Himself. What did He empty Himself of? He emptied Himself of His prerogatives of deity. As He left heaven's glory and stepped out of that domain, countless numbers of angels, myriads of God's created intelligences, fell down and worshiped Him. But when He got to this earth, what happened? There were a few little, insignificant shepherds—that's all. The bulk of mankind on this earth was falling down and worshiping Caesar Augustus; and from Caesar Augustus to Hitler, they still worship men. Christ emptied Himself of His prerogatives of deity, His rights, His glory. Why? That He might take on Himself our form.

The infinite God came down and became a man! Why? Because man is a sinner. He has to be judged and pushed out of God's presence, or God will have to lift him up. That's the only way back.

Now I move into a realm I know nothing about—music. I'm told that on our pipe organ there are four major stops. Oh, there are forty or fifty stops altogether, but there are four major stops. One is known as "diapason," another is known as "flute," another as "strings," and the fourth is *vox humana* (human voice). I'm told that very few organs have a *vox humana* because it almost always is out of tune. Change the temperature of the room even slightly and your *vox humana* will be off-key.

May I say, the Creator of this universe stepped to the organ of His creation, He pulled out the stop "diapason," and the firmament gave forth the glory of God! He pulled out the "flute" stop: "Praise Him with the sound of the trumpet; praise Him with the lute and harp!" (Psalm 150:3). He pulled out the "string" stop: "Praise Him with the timbrel and dance; praise Him with stringed instruments and flutes!" (Psalm 150:4). Then He pulled out *vox humana*. It was out of tune—there was no response.

So He left heaven's glory. He came down to this earth to bring *vox humana* back in tune with heaven. And patiently today God—the Creator of this universe, the infinite God—though high above us, is dealing with mankind! The reason He is high above us is because our sins have separated us from God. But He has made a way back, and that way back is through Christ who died on the cross to redeem us.

CHAPTER 3

WHAT DOES GOD LOOK LIKE?

Pierre-Simon Laplace, the French astronomer, said years ago, "I have searched the heavens with a telescope, and I did not see God." Dr. Sawyer, an astronomer of equal greatness and also a very wonderful Christian, said of Laplace's attempt to see God, "He might as well have swept the kitchen with a broom." In other words, "What a waste of time!" May I say that you and I are never going to see God sticking His head around one of the planets or one of the stars or out yonder in one of the galactic systems. No instrument of science crafted by the human hand is capable of deciphering the impenetrable mysteries of our God. From out of the clouds and darkness that are around God's throne, the question comes,

Can you search out the deep things of God? Can you find out the limits of the Almighty? (Job 11:7)

Therefore, I am confident that I shall not be able to answer the question to the satisfaction of every person: "What does God look like?"

One night a little girl began to fret and cry upstairs in her bed, and her mother went to her and said, "What's the matter, honey?" The child answered, "I'm afraid up here by myself." Her mother wanted to encourage her, so she said, "Well, God's up here with you." The little girl replied, "Yes, I know, but I want somebody with a face." Well, we all want somebody with a face. So why is it that we have not seen Him? Why is there this inability to see God? For there is an axiom of Scripture that says,

> **No one has seen God at any time. The only begotten Son, who is in the bosom of the Father, He has declared Him** [that is, brought Him out in the open where men can see Him]. (John 1:18)

"No one has seen God at any time." That's true in the Old Testament, it's true in the New Testament, and it's true today.

I may be wrong, but through studying the Book of Revelation I have come to the conclusion that we may never see God—not even throughout the endless ages of eternity. I believe that we shall see the Lord Jesus Christ—we shall be *with* Him—and the Father is there, but whether or not you and I are going to *see* the Father, I'm not too sure.

Someone is bound to say, "Wait just a minute. It says in the Old Testament that certain men did see God. What about that?" Well, we are told in Genesis 32:24,

> **Then Jacob was left alone; and a Man wrestled with him until the breaking of day.**

Now we shouldn't interpret that to mean that Jacob wanted to wrestle the Man. To begin with, he had his angry father-in-law to deal with, and also his brother who had threatened to kill him was after him. Do you think he wanted to take on a third person that night? No. The Scripture says the Man wrestled *with Jacob*. But when the sun arose and the struggling was finished, we read:

> **So Jacob called the name of the place Peniel: "For I have seen God face to face, and my life is preserved."** (Genesis 32:30)

Whom did Jacob see? The record is clear: There wrestled *a Man* with Jacob. But who was the

Man? I personally believe it was the pre-incarnate Christ. But whether or not I am correct in my thesis, Jacob did not see God! All he saw was the Man who wrestled with him. He did not see God.

Someone else may ask, "Well, all right, Jacob didn't see God. But what about Moses? Didn't Moses see God?" Notice Exodus 33:18–19:

> **And he said, "Please, show me Your glory." Then He said, "I will make all My goodness pass before you, and I will proclaim the name of the LORD before you. I will be gracious to whom I will be gracious, and I will have compassion on whom I will have compassion."**

God made it clear to Moses that what He was doing wasn't because Moses was the leader or because Moses had done something outstanding. Rather, when God does anything, He does it because there's no respect of persons with Him. God is sovereign. If God wants to be gracious, He will be gracious; if God wants to show mercy, He will show mercy. And you have no right to question Him. Never say He's wrong in what He's doing. Our God is doing things right, my beloved, and it's time believers defended Him instead of questioning Him! So the Lord said to Moses, "Moses, I'm going to give you an unusual experience. I will let you see something no man has ever seen. But I want you to know that this is not because you're a leader or because you've done something to deserve it. It's because I'm extending mercy to you, and I'm being gracious to you." Now notice in verse 20:

> **But He said, "You cannot see My face; for no man shall see Me, and live."**

He hid Moses in the cleft of the rock, and He made His glory pass by. But Moses did not *see* God! It's still an axiom for both the Old and New Testaments, "No one has seen God at any time."

Again, why can we not see God? The Scripture, I think, gives the answer to that. Our Lord said,

> **God is Spirit, and those who worship Him must worship in spirit and truth.** (John 4:24)

The original Greek reads, "God is Spirit"; or even better still, *pneuma ho theos*—"Spirit is God." God is essential and, in essence, God is Spirit. God is not material; therefore He is not dependent on material things in this universe. That is to say, He doesn't need air to breathe, and He does not rely on any kind of nourishment to survive. God can see, but He doesn't have eyes; He can hear, but He doesn't have ears. A poet put it like this:

There is an eye that never sleeps beneath the
   wing of night.
There is an ear that never shuts when sink the
   beams of light.
There is an arm that never tires when human
   strength gives way.
There is a love that never fails when earthly
   loves decay.
That eye unseen o'er watcheth all; that arm
   upholds the sky.
That ear doth hear the sparrow's call; that love
   is ever nigh.

(Author unknown)

I recognize that this is a difficult concept to
grasp. We are dealing with an infinite God, and
because we are only finite creatures it's very difficult for us to think of God as being Spirit. I am
reminded of the story about the boy who was trying to explain wireless telegraphy to his friend
who couldn't understand how it worked. The boy
said to his friend, "Now, it's like this: Say you
have a long dog. That dog is so long that its tail is
in Memphis and its head is over in Birmingham.
If you step on his tail in Memphis, he barks over
in Birmingham!" My beloved, wireless telegraphy
is difficult to understand. And, likewise, it's a real
difficulty to understand that God is Spirit. But
I'm going to try to make it simple so that we all
can grasp it.

You see, man is only partially physical. We have certain senses—every one of them is a physical sense. We have an eye-gate, an ear-gate, we have taste buds, and we have hands that can feel cold and heat. We come in contact with the physical universe with these bodies of ours. We need the material, the physical, to establish a conscious existence. But we are also spiritual creatures, and there's a mingling of the physical and spiritual in man. The psalmist was right when he wrote:

I will praise You, for I am fearfully and wonderfully made; marvelous are Your works, and that my soul knows very well. (Psalm 139:14)

God, on the other hand, is not physical. He is Spirit. We need eyes in order to see, but God sees without eyes. We need ears in order to hear, but God hears without ears. He made the eye, and the One who made the eye can see. He made the ear, and the One who made the ear can hear. This is not easy for us to understand, so the Word of God uses what is known as anthropomorphic terms. That's a big word, but it's really a very simple word: *Anthropo* means "man" and *morphic* means "shape or form." It means that terms that apply to man are used to describe God so that you and I can understand difficult concepts. I cannot understand how a spirit can see. I'm sorry, but I just don't get it. But when I read, "The eyes of the LORD run to and fro throughout the whole earth" (2 Chronicles 16:9), I understand it means that God sees everything, that without eyes He is able to do what I'm able to do with them. I have to wear bifocals, but even though God is the Ancient of Days He doesn't need glasses and still sees better than I do.

The psalmist gives another example:

The heavens declare the glory of God; and the firmament shows His handiwork.
(Psalm 19:1)

Creating this tremendous universe did not take all of the strength and power and ability of God. It was merely handiwork to Him; it was just a little crocheting, if you will. Someone has said, "God created a universe and didn't even half try." When He rested on the seventh day it wasn't because He was tired. He had simply completed the job, and there was nothing else to be done on it. It was a rest of completeness and perfection—the kind of rest He wants you and me to enter into when we come to Christ. Christ did it all, and so we enter into the sabbath rest. I never complete anything. I have never left my study saying that everything is finished. But when God finished creating the universe, it was *complete*. The amazing thing, though, is that it was just "handiwork" to Him.

But when God was ready to redeem man, it wasn't handiwork. In Isaiah 53:1 we read:

To whom has the arm of the LORD been revealed?

Isaiah is not speaking here of a physical arm; he is making a contrast. Saying that God has an arm and that He does handiwork is the only way we can understand that it cost God more to redeem man than it did to create a universe. You are more important to Him than the universe. He used His fingers to create a universe; but when He redeemed you, a sinner, it was with His bared arm. No, He doesn't really have fingers, and He doesn't have an arm. But that's the only way we will ever understand it.

God is nonmaterial. Material is His creation, and therefore it's beneath Him; it's not part of Him at all:

Therefore, since we are the offspring of God, we ought not to think that the Divine Nature is like gold or silver or stone, something shaped by art and man's devising. (Acts 17:29)

This is the reason that from the very beginning God forbade man to make any image or likeness of Him. From the word *go* God said:

You shall not make for yourself any carved image, or any likeness of anything that is in heaven above, or that is in the earth beneath, or that is in the water under the earth; you shall not bow down to them nor serve them. For I, the LORD your God, am a jealous God, visiting the iniquity of the fathers on the children to the third and fourth generations of those who hate Me. (Exodus 20:4–5)

He also asked the question,

To whom will you liken Me, and make Me equal and compare Me, that we should be alike? (Isaiah 46:5)

In other words, "Whom do you think I look like?" No one could ever make a true likeness of Him, because God is Spirit.

In spite of His repeated warnings to the Israelites to stay away from idolatry, they would not listen. Eventually their disobedience sent them into captivity. The story of the human family is not one of evolution up to God, but it is a story of devolution from a knowledge of God:

Because, although they knew God, they did not glorify Him as God, nor were thankful, but became futile in their

**thoughts, and their foolish hearts were
darkened.** (Romans 1:21)

People began to make likenesses of four-footed
creatures, of the sun and the moon and the stars,
of just about everything, and began to worship
them. Paul went into the city of Athens and said
in effect, you have worshiped *everything*, and now
you've even put up an image to an "unknown
god." You recognize the fact that there is a God
you do not know, and I want to tell you about
Him. Now notice what God said to the nation
Israel:

**Take careful heed to yourselves, for you
saw no form when the LORD spoke to you
at Horeb out of the midst of the fire, lest
you act corruptly and make for yourselves a carved image in the form of any
figure: the likeness of male or female, the
likeness of any animal that is on the earth
or the likeness of any winged bird that
flies in the air, the likeness of anything
that creeps on the ground or the likeness
of any fish that is in the water beneath
the earth. And take heed, lest you lift your
eyes to heaven, and when you see the sun,
the moon, and the stars, all the host of
heaven, you feel driven to worship them
and serve them, which the LORD your God**

has given to all the peoples under the whole heaven as a heritage. (Deuteronomy 4:15–19)

May I say to you, God's warning to His people was repeated again and again, and still today He forbids us to make an image. The reason is because God is not like these things made of silver and gold; He doesn't look like that at all. God is Spirit, and any likeness or representation of Him is wrong, whether it be a totem pole, an idol of Baal, a statue of Zeus, a sitting Buddha, or a plaster-of-paris saint. Those things are wrong! God says, "Make nothing that represents Me."

Although God is Spirit, two thousand years ago He broke through into human history and took upon Himself human flesh. Our Lord Jesus Christ was God in the flesh.

Philip said to Him, "Lord, show us the Father, and it is sufficient for us." Jesus said to him, "Have I been with you so long, and yet you have not known Me, Philip? He who has seen Me has seen the Father." (John 14:8–9)

But are we ever told what Jesus looked like? No. I cannot find in any one of the Gospels that there was born to Mary a nine-pound baby boy with blue eyes and light hair or brown eyes and dark hair. A description of Him is not given in Scripture, and that is why our human attempts to paint a picture of Christ are not accurate. Oh, I know, all of those beautiful paintings are lovely to look at—the only thing is that Christ didn't look like a single one of them.

Thomas Carlyle, a Scottish philosopher, said that men never think of painting an image of Christ until they've lost the impression of Him on their hearts. Now, I know this won't go over well with a great many people—especially those who run Christian bookstores—but I think it's wrong to use pictures of Christ today! "Oh," someone is sure to say, "I have a little altar in my living room. I've put a picture of Jesus up there, and I like to go and pray before it." If that's true, then you're nothing in the world but an idolater! "But," the person might argue, "I need that to help me." Friend, if you know Him as your Savior, you do not need a picture of Him to help you. I know that's not a popular opinion today. I was at a retreat some time ago and while I was there I went into the bookstore. I watched the people as they came in to shop, and some of them bought my books that were for sale there. But the thing that bothered me was that they bought twice as many of the little plaster-of-paris figurines of Christ. But do you know that none of those folks could say that's what Jesus really looked like?

Isn't it interesting that nothing physical that

was connected to Him has survived? God made sure of that. Someone who was telling me about his visit to Palestine said, "I went to the Garden Tomb, and it was so awesome I just got down on my knees and had a wonderful prayer." My thought about that was, *You mean you had to make a trip to Palestine to have a wonderful prayer?*

It seems that we are developing a group of Protestants who are running around looking for sacred spots and pictures and that sort of thing. Oh, my friend, have you lost the Savior? Why do you have to have these things today?

No, we have no way of knowing what God looks like, but there are two all-important characteristics of God that we can know something about. The first, as we've already seen, is that God is Spirit. The second is that He is a person. You may be asking, "How can a spirit have personality?" Now just because God is Spirit does not mean that He's not a person. You don't have to possess a physical body to be a person. For instance, Scripture makes it very clear that what you and I live in today, this physical body, is passing away. It's only temporary. Paul said,

For we know that if our earthly house, this tent, is destroyed, we have a building from God, a house not made with hands, eternal in the heavens. (2 Corinthians 5:1)

John Quincy Adams was a great man and a wonderful Christian. When he was an old man a friend met him in the street and asked, "How are you, Mr. Adams?" He answered, "I'm very well, but this house I live in is becoming mighty feeble." This body that I'm living in is only a house—it is not who I am as a person.

We often make the mistake of associating a person with the body he lives in instead of seeing the person he is on the inside. However, sometimes the real personality comes to the surface. For example, have you ever been driving down the freeway and come across someone in the next lane who just will not move over and let you in? I've observed these people and nine out of ten of them have the same stubborn mouth. You see, sometimes our personalities do come out and show themselves in our physical bodies. But our bodies themselves do not make us who we are and, for the most part, do not reflect what kind of people we are.

Now, I've said that God has personality while at the same time being Spirit. You may ask: What is your definition of a person? It's one who is capable of self-consciousness and self-determination. Animals are conscious, but they are not self-conscious. You see a man and a dog going down the street. The dog is just conscious—the only thing on his mind is when he'll eat next. But the man is aware of himself—who he is, where he is going, what he is going to do once he gets there. Little babies are not self-conscious, though. They have no inhibitions whatsoever. As we grow older we become aware of ourselves. But you know, friends, the unusual thing is that we're not always self-conscious. Sometimes we come to ourselves all of a sudden as the prodigal son did. One day he woke up and said, "I'm a son of my father. What am I doing down in this pigpen? I'm going home!" He became self-conscious real quick and got out of that pigpen.

Every now and then a man (and he's got to be an intelligent fellow to do this) will ask himself, "Who am I? Where am I going? What am I doing in this life?" Do you have answers to those questions? Who are you? Have you realized that you're a sinner—lost, hell-doomed, and on the way to a Christless eternity? Have you discovered that a Savior died for you and that as an intelligent being you can come to Him? Do you know who you are today? Do you know where you're headed? Oh, how many men and women today need to wake up, get a little sense, and ask the questions, "Who am I? Where am I going?"

God knows exactly who He is. He said to Moses at the very beginning,

I AM WHO I AM. (Exodus 3:14)

God recognizes Himself, and He acts rationally because He knows who He is. He doesn't have anyone to compare Himself to as we do, but He says, "I am who I am—I am God!"

The second thing that determines personality is self-determination. I once heard a definition that whatever has its cause outside of itself is a thing, and that which has its cause within itself is a person. If you see a parked car with no one in it, it's just a thing. You put somebody at the wheel, and it's altogether different. Now the car has somebody to determine where it will go. A person has the ability to decide. The inanimate world, on the other hand, is governed by laws—the laws of gravity and so forth—over which it has no control. Take this book that you are holding. It has a lot of sense in it, but it has no sense of itself—it's inanimate. It's not thinking to itself, *Please don't drop me.* This book has no control whatsoever. Likewise, the brute world outside is governed by instinct. In the winter the ducks and geese up in Canada fly south. And when they do, the old gander doesn't say to the goose, "Our vacation is about over; we'll be leaving now in two weeks. Have you packed your suitcase, and is little gosling ready to fly?" Do you think any of those concerns ever come to his mind? Not on your life! One day the old gander just starts out, and even though none of those little goslings have ever been south before, they all follow. Some may get lost from the flock, but they will find their way to that warm winter habitat. Can you tell me how they do it? It's by instinct; those geese don't have any choice in the matter at all. It happens by instinct.

May I say to you, my beloved, the power of choice is limited to mankind. We have been given the power to choose. When we come to a crossroad we have to make a decision as to which way we'll go. For instance, you decided to pick up this book and start reading. Maybe you decided you might benefit from reading it, or someone else did and so gave it to you. We are self-conscious beings, and we make choices accordingly. Of course, I recognize that the power to choose is limited, but generally we have that ability.

Now, we've determined that God is self-conscious, and He also has the ultimate power to choose and decide. So it is obvious to us that God possesses the qualities to make Him a person. And because He is a person we can know Him and talk to Him personally. In the Old Testament it says,

So the LORD spoke to Moses face to face, as a man speaks to his friend. (Exodus 33:11)

Why face to face? Because God is a person. God spoke as an intelligent Creator to this intelligent creature whom He had made.

God is also life. That doesn't mean that God merely *has* life, but He *is* life. I'm not quibbling over terms now. He breathes out life, and everything that has life must draw it from Him. His personality is never diminished or decreased because He gives out life. The Old Testament makes it clear that He is the living God, and everything else that is worshiped is a dead god. Jeremiah said to his people who had turned to idolatry,

> **But the LORD is the true God; He is the living God and the everlasting King.** (Jeremiah 10:10)

And old Elijah chided the prophets of Baal, "Where's your god? He must be asleep. He doesn't hear you." Baal couldn't hear them because he was an idol made by the hand of man. Only the living God hears! In the New Testament Paul said to the Thessalonians,

> **. . . You turned to God from idols to serve the living and true God.** (1 Thessalonians 1:9)

And the Lord Jesus Christ said when He was here,

> **I am the way, the truth, and the life. No one comes to the Father except through Me.** (John 14:6)

Christ is the living God and the life-giver, and He lives eternally. However, our lives today are subject to time. Time is God's creation, so He is not affected by it. When Paul speaks about things separating us from God, he says,

> **For I am persuaded that neither death nor life, nor angels nor principalities nor powers, *nor things present nor things to come,* nor height nor depth, nor any other created thing, shall be able to separate us from the love of God which is in Christ Jesus our Lord.** (Romans 8:38–39, emphasis mine)

Time is His creation, and although it affects us in physical ways, time does not affect God. It writes no wrinkle on His brow; it plows no furrow in His cheek; it puts no gray in His hair. He is the Ancient of Days, but He is ever young for He lives in eternity. We are frail creatures of time. It affects us like a disease, and it shows itself in the wrinkles on our faces and the frailness of our bodies. I like the way the Bible speaks of Abraham's death. It says when Abraham died, he was "one hundred and seventy-five years . . . an old man and full of years" (Genesis 25:7–8). What did Abraham die of? He was full of years!

The apostle Peter states that God is not subject to time. He says,

> **But, beloved, do not forget this one thing, that with the Lord one day is as a thou-**

sand years, and a thousand years as one day. (2 Peter 3:8)

Sinclair Lewis, an agnostic novelist, walked to the edge of the Grand Canyon, held his watch in his hand, and said, "If there be a God let Him strike me dead in five minutes." All of the people who admired and followed the writings of Sinclair Lewis stood around breathless. And as you may know, nothing happened in five minutes. So Sinclair Lewis turned around to the crowd and said, "See, there is no God." I can't think of anything more absurd than that and, as some wag said, "He was looking at the wrong clock." Sinclair Lewis lived for several years after that incident at the Grand Canyon. But do you know that he died in five minutes according to God's clock, where a thousand years is a day and a day is a thousand years? He did die in five minutes— he was just looking at the wrong clock!

A great many people are looking at the wrong timepiece. Perhaps you're one of them, and you say, "I've got plenty of time." But you are wrong, my friend. Only God has plenty of time today. Only He has time on His hands, if you please! Man is like the grass of the field. Man lives only a moment of time; our lives are like one drop of water from a bucket. But God lives eternally—all of time pressed into one moment! That's the reason He knows the end from the beginning. How is that possible? Because our God is Spirit.

May I say that today there are a great many people saying, "Show us God." Remember that the Lord Jesus said, "He who has seen Me has seen the Father" (John 14:9). There are multitudes of people who would like to know God. They're rather skeptical because they cannot see Him with their eyes. But if they could only see Christ in you and me, they would know Him. That's the real problem today. If they could only see Christ in us!

My friend, if you are without Christ today and you're just waiting for Him to meet you when you turn the corner, it will not happen. You won't see Him that way:

God is Spirit, and those who worship Him must worship in spirit and truth.
(John 4:24)

You and I are finite; He is infinite. But two thousand years ago He left heaven's glory to come down here to become a man—a person—so that we might know Him personally.

I don't know what God looks like today, but I can still know Him. I turn the pages of Scripture and read about my lovely Lord. I see Him weeping at the tomb of Lazarus, and I know that's the way God feels about death. I see Him going into a home and restoring the life of a little girl because He wants to keep the family intact. I see Him feeding five thousand hungry men, besides women and children, and I know how God feels about the multitudes in places like India where people are hungry every day. No, we do not know what He looks like, but God can be known today by what He has done for you and me.

And this is eternal life, that they may know You, the only true God, and Jesus Christ whom You have sent. (John 17:3)

You can know Him as the One who died on the cross for your sin. You can know Him as your Savior. Paul, at the end of his life, said,

That I may know Him and the power of His resurrection, and the fellowship of His sufferings, being conformed to His death. (Philippians 3:10)

It does not matter that no one has seen His face, because you have been given enough information about God to make an intelligent decision! He is a person as well as Spirit, so He understands that the choice is up to you. He will not barge in on you and destroy your personality. He made you as you are, and He has given to you the power to choose:

But as many as received Him, to them He gave the right to become children of God, even to those who believe in His name. (John 1:12)

You can know Him as your Savior.

CHAPTER 4

DOES A GOD
OF LOVE HATE?

A poet wrote about the reports in the Monday paper on the variety of sermons that had been preached in various churches on Sunday morning:

> On page twenty-seven, just opposite "Fashion
>   Trends,"
> One reads at a glance how He scolded the
>   Baptists a little,
> Was firm with the Catholics, practical with the
>   Friends;
> For the Unitarians He was pleasantly non-
>   committal.
> Always on Monday morning, the press reports
> God as revealed to His vicars in various guises;
> Benevolent, stormy, patient, or out of sorts,
> God knows which god is the god God recognizes.
>   (Author unknown)

This little poem reveals that churchgoers are getting a garbled God and a diversified Deity from the contemporary pulpit. Under the guise of wanting to know God better, the modern pulpit has attempted to pull God from His throne, where He sits high above the heavens, and put Him down in the mud and mire of the commonplace. The argument made is that the only way to know God better is to bring Him down to our low level so that we can rub shoulders with Him, so to speak. This practice mistakes familiarity with God for a true knowledge of Him. When we are ignorant of who God is, we think we can take unwarrantable liberties with Him. I heard about one speaker at a young people's conference who said he would like to paint a portrait of Jesus wearing a sports shirt. I say to you that you can't paint Jesus in a sports shirt! To begin with,

Even though we have known Christ according to the flesh, yet now we know Him thus no longer. (2 Corinthians 5:16)

And John, when he was granted a vision of the post-incarnate Christ, said: "And when I saw Him, I fell at His feet as dead" (Revelation 1:17). John was the disciple closest to Jesus; he was the man who reclined on Jesus' bosom in the Upper Room. Yet when he saw the glorified Christ, he fell at His feet as dead. My friend, if John reacted like that, how can you and I assume a casual familiarity with Him? Any attempt to bring God down and to become familiar with Him is a very dangerous thing. It makes people believe that our God is One with whom you can take liberties and that He's just a buddy or an old man reclining on a cloud. But those conceptions of Him are not true. God says to us:

> You thought that I was altogether like you; but I will rebuke you, and set them in order before your eyes. (Psalm 50:21)

God is not like man. Isaiah, who was the amanuensis for God, wrote:

> "For My thoughts are not your thoughts, nor are your ways My ways," says the LORD. "For as the heavens are higher than the earth, so are My ways higher than your ways, and My thoughts than your thoughts." (Isaiah 55:8–9)

But if God is not like us, what is He like?

Scripture gives us three definitions of God, and we need all of them to have a correct perspective of Him. We are told that God is Spirit, God is light, and God is love. These are not, by the way, characteristics of God. But God is precisely what these terms connote: God *is* Spirit; God *is* light; God *is* love. In other words, these are comprehensive descriptions of God, and we need to hold them in balance or we're apt to get a wrong impression of Him.

God Is Spirit

First, our God is Spirit:

> **God is Spirit, and those who worship Him must worship in spirit and truth.** (John 4:24)

Actually, the original Greek text says it even better: *pneuma ho theos*, or "Spirit is God." We covered this in detail when we were on the subject of what God looks like, so we won't dwell on this too long. But notice that it does not say God is *a* Spirit—the *a* is not there. It clearly says that God *is* Spirit. He had to become flesh—become one of us—in order for us to know Him. Man could not become spirit to know Him, so He became like us:

> **And the Word became flesh and dwelt among us, and we beheld His glory, the glory as of the only begotten of the Father, full of grace and truth.** (John 1:14)

Jesus Christ came to this earth as God in the flesh so that we might know Him and come to God personally. But, essentially, God is Spirit.

God Is Light

The next definition of God is that He is light. Notice what John says:

This is the message which we have heard from Him and declare to you, that God is light and in Him is no darkness at all. (1 John 1:5)

Now, John is not referring to physical light, although I believe that physical light is part of it. The verse actually means that God is holy.

Not only is He holy, but His holiness is perfect and intransitive—it is a light with no darkness at all. James says:

Every good gift and every perfect gift is from above, and comes down from the Father of lights, with whom there is no variation or shadow of turning. (James 1:17)

In God there is no dark side; He does not cast a shadow. Man, on the other hand, does. In fact, that's all we do. None of us are light-bearers; in all of us there is a shadow. It is said that when Alexander the Great returned from his world tour of victory, he came back to his hometown and went to the home of his teacher, Aristotle. When he arrived, Aristotle was taking a bath, and

Alexander rushed right in where he was bathing. Alexander the Great said, "I've conquered the world, and I'd like to give you anything that you want. What would you like to have?" Aristotle just kept on with his bath and said, "All I'd like is for you to get out of my light!" In Aristotle's opinion, Alexander the Great was just a body casting a shadow on his light. And that's what we do, too. But God is light and so He does not cast a shadow at all. His holiness is perfect.

May I say this lifts God up and separates Him from His creation today. His holiness, among other things, sets Him apart from mankind because:

No one is holy like the LORD, for there is none besides You, nor is there any rock like our God. (1 Samuel 2:2)

He is so holy that the Book of Job (probably the first book written in the Bible) says:

If God puts no trust in His saints, and the heavens are not pure in His sight, how much less man, who is abominable and filthy, who drinks iniquity like water! (Job 15:15–16)

That's how holy our God is. But there is more—listen to Habakkuk who said:

> You are of purer eyes than to behold
> evil, and cannot look on wickedness.
> (Habakkuk 1:13)

Friends, a holy God cannot look upon evil and iniquity, and therefore He is separated from us. That is why our sin must be confessed and forgiven before we can be accepted by Him.

We've lost that sense of God's holiness. We think that, somehow or another, God is being very tolerant with sin and with evil. May I say to you that we cannot find one situation from Genesis to Revelation in which God compromises with sin or evil. Neither in the Old Testament nor the New Testament has God lowered His standard one iota, and He will never lower that standard! God is holy, and He demands holiness of His people.

This is an important lesson. In fact, I would say it's the all-important lesson that He taught His people in the Old Testament. He had a great deal of difficulty getting this truth through to them, which is the reason we find minutiae and meticulous rituals in the Old Testament. The Book of Leviticus is without doubt one of the most monotonous books in the Bible, and yet it's the most wonderful book if you get its message. Have you ever noticed how many times the words *clean* and *unclean* are used? God says to His people over and over again: This is clean; that is unclean;

cleanse yourself here; don't cleanse yourself there. The reason they were to do all of this is also given and repeated; it was because "I am the LORD your God" (see Leviticus 19). God said to His people,

Speak to all the congregation of the children of Israel, and say to them: "You shall be holy, for I the LORD your God am holy." (Leviticus 19:2)

That is all the reason we should need, my beloved. We are to be holy because He is holy.

By requiring Old Testament ceremonies, God was teaching His people that He is holy and that He requires holiness of those who belong to Him. My, how they went through ceremonies in the Old Testament! The high priest came to the tabernacle, and then later to the temple, and wore out his hands washing them. He washed them before he served, he washed them afterward, and then he washed his feet. He couldn't take one step inside the Holy Place without washing his feet. Why all of that? So the people would know that God is holy and that He demands holiness of His people.

Now, the Pharisees in Jesus' day missed the meaning of all the cleansing. They were meticulous in every detail of the observance of the Law. They would not eat with unwashed hands, and when they saw the disciples of our Lord eating with unwashed hands, they were absolutely horrified. Our Lord told them that they had missed the meaning of the Law. It wasn't a question, actually, of eating with washed or unwashed hands:

Not what goes into the mouth defiles a man; but what comes out of the mouth, this defiles a man. (Matthew 15:11)

God gave these laws to show that His people had to be holy, because that is the only way of coming into God's presence. You see, there was a purpose behind the ceremonial cleansing, but they had missed it.

God has not changed in the New Testament; He is still a holy God. In that wonderful seventeenth chapter of John, where the Lord Jesus prays what I believe is the real "Lord's Prayer," we hear Him praying for those down here on earth whom the Father had given Him. Have you noticed how, when He becomes intimate, He addresses the Father as "Holy Father"?:

Holy Father, keep through Your name those whom You have given Me, that they may be one as We are. (v. 11)

Later on in His prayer He calls Him,

O righteous Father! The world has not known You, but I have known You; and these have known that You sent Me. (v. 25)

That is the thing that has not changed as far as the believer is concerned today. Our God is *holy* and He is *righteous*. Because of that He is separated from lowly man. In order to draw us close to Him, He must demand the same of us. Paul, writing to the Thessalonians, said:

For God did not call us to uncleanness, but in holiness. (1 Thessalonians 4:7)

But today we've forgotten that God has called us to holiness, that our uncleanness is not accepted by Him. God will not fellowship with sin, my friend. Never, never will He fellowship with sin. He is holy, and that fact has never changed.

It is important also to understand that holiness is not merely a quality of God. It is not an adornment, an accessory; nor is it an accoutrement. May I say to you, it's the *character* of God that is holy. Notice the fine distinction: It's not His conduct, it's His character. It's in God's character to be holy. He didn't have to train Himself. It's the *nature* of God! It's in the web and woof of His being! God is holy, and if He were not holy then He would not be God. It's something that He *is*. He *is* holy.

Some people try to be cultured and educated, and they make a great effort at it. They read Emily Post and struggle at trying to use the right knife and fork. I remember hearing Dr. Lewis

Sperry Chafer say years ago that the best thing to do is to *be* cultured and educated, and then all you have to do is act naturally. My family was invited to have dinner one night in a home where the wife and mother was a graduate of a local finishing school for girls. We took notice of the hospitality and culture of that woman's home. She wasn't trying to put on airs; she was acting naturally. That's the way she is all of the time. May I repeat, God doesn't *try* to be holy. God *is* holy.

Also, the holiness of God is positive and active. Light illuminates the darkness to reveal flaws and impurities; when one turns on the light, all the rats, bats, and bedbugs crawl away. Light not only reveals that which is hidden in the darkness, but light consumes the darkness. Just as light and darkness cannot exist at the same time, neither can holiness and evil coexist. The writer to the Hebrews declared: "For our God is a consuming fire" (Hebrews 12:29). Just as the fire destroys the chaff, so does God's holiness consume evil. This explains the actions of God with His people. He is holy, and because He is holy His conduct must be righteous and just.

God is righteous in everything that He does, and He is just in everything that He does. For example, God is righteous when He demands conformity. He says, "You shall therefore be holy, for I am holy" (Leviticus 11:45). God doesn't lower that standard for anyone. Do you think you are going to get into heaven without holiness? Well, you won't. God is righteous when He demands holiness, and He is just when He exacts a penalty for failure!

Now, justice demands that He punish the guilty. Listen to Paul:

> **But in accordance with your hardness and your impenitent heart you are treasuring up for yourself wrath in the day of wrath and revelation of the righteous judgment of God, who "will render to each one according to his deeds."** (Romans 2:5–6)

He's not speaking here to down-and-outers on skid row. Actually, he's speaking to rather "cultured" sinners, and yet he still says that God will judge every man according to his deeds. Do you want to stand before God on that basis? He will not judge you by only your good deeds, but He will judge you on the total deeds of your life—good and bad. He has to do that because God is righteous, God is just, and He must judge man on that basis!

Many of us have a problem with this. Let's look to Abraham, because he had a problem with this, too. God told Abraham that He was going to destroy Sodom and Gomorrah because their sin was very great. Abraham responded with a question that a great many people today would ask:

> Far be it from You to do such a thing as this,
> to slay the righteous with the wicked, so
> that the righteous should be as the wicked;
> far be it from You! Shall not the Judge of all
> the earth do right? (Genesis 18:25)

In other words, Abraham said, "You don't mean to
tell me that You are going to destroy the righteous
of Sodom and Gomorrah along with the wicked?" As
you know, my friend, we don't really mean it when
we say we want God to be just in what He does.
What we really want is for God to be merciful. So
God answered Abraham, saying that if fifty
righteous could be found within the city, Sodom
and Gomorrah would be spared. Then Abraham
began to barter, and he got the Lord down to ten.
Why did Abraham stop at ten? Well, his nephew
Lot was in Sodom, and Abraham started to get a
little worried about him. But do you know that
Abraham could have come all the way down to just
one? The reason I know that is because that's how
it happened. There was one righteous person in the
city—Lot—and God said to him, "Get out of the city,
Lot, because I cannot destroy it until you are out."

The Judge of all the earth is holy, and He
always does what is right and just.

> What shall we say then? Is there unrigh-
> teousness with God? Certainly not!
> (Romans 9:14)

Whatever God does is right, and if you don't think He is right, the trouble is not with God but with you and your thinking. You do not have all the facts or all the details. If you did, you would know that the Judge of all the earth does right. God does not have a feeling of guilt about judging Sodom and Gomorrah, nor does He wonder if He was right in sending the Flood in Noah's day. He is a holy and just God, One who has not and never will shut His eyes to sin. We are the ones who are wrong; He is right.

God is light; and since God is light, He is holy; and since God is holy, He is purity; and since God is purity, He will not compromise with sin. God is at war with sin! In the Song of Moses, when the Israelites crossed the Red Sea, Moses said, "The LORD is a man of war; the LORD is His name" (Exodus 15:3). We don't like to acknowledge that fact in our day, but it happens to be true. God loves the good, but He hates sin! Paul said about believers:

> **For we must all appear before the judgment seat of Christ, that each one may receive the things done in the body, according to what he has done, whether good or bad. Knowing, therefore, the terror of the Lord, we persuade men . . . .**
> (2 Corinthians 5:10–11)

If you think as a child of God you're getting by with sin, you're dead wrong. You are dealing with a God who is holy and just. If you think He doesn't care about your sin or makes light of it, you are saying that He is not holy, that He is not righteous and just in His dealings. But He *is* holy and just, and He has plenty of time to call you to account.

God Is Love

Now, let's move to the next definition of God: "God is love." In 1 John 4:8 we are told:

He who does not love does not know God, for God is love.

God *is* love in the same way that He *is* Spirit and He *is* holy; there are absolutely no limits or boundaries to it. That means God loves infinitely. You and I cannot comprehend how wonderful and glorious His love is. But I must add here that the love of God has been exaggerated and presented in a lopsided manner in our day. There has been an overstatement of the love of God at the expense of His other attributes. May I say to you, it's the same as cutting a dog's tail off behind the ears—too much else is lost! The modern notion of God's love has been so stretched out of proportion that it is now perceived as the saccharine sweetness of a dear, harmless old lady sitting in a corner, knitting. In my judgment there is nothing in liberal theology so nauseating as the idea that God's love is so great and unparticular that it just slops over on all sides. Overemphasizing God's love makes it bland, flavorless, colorless, and downright mediocre. The true magnificence and indescribable wonder of His love are lost in all the padding that liberal theologians have added.

I want you to see what I mean by that. So often I hear the expression, "God loves the sinner, but He hates the sin." Have you heard that? I've heard it even from visiting speakers in my pulpit. That is a fallacy. That's not the way the Word of God reads, my beloved. Here is what it does say:

**The boastful shall not stand in Your sight;
You hate all workers of iniquity.** (Psalm 5:5)

We like to separate the sin from the sinner and let God judge only the sin, but God judges the sinner:

**God is a just judge, and God is angry with
the wicked every day.** (Psalm 7:11)

Yes, our God is a God who hates sin. Yes, He loves the sinner. But He hates the sinner who holds on to sin, for that sinner must bear the *wrath* of God someday. Thomas Fuller likened it to saying that you can starve the profanity of the beggar but still feed the person of the beggar. My friend, you can't starve the profanity of the beggar who is cursing God! When you feed the body, you feed the profanity and all the rest along with it. And God will judge the sinner who holds on to sin because God *hates* sin, and He hates the sinner who holds on to it.

I'm now moving into an area that's brand-new to many people. Will you follow me very carefully? We've had our thinking colored by this flabby and flashy age in which we live, and we've had "cream puff" and "French pastry" theology spoon-fed to us for a long time. The modern pulpit has been spewing humid and hot humanism, pious platitudes, and despicable double-talk that have led to spiritual suicide for multitudes of people.

Love is not supreme in the attributes of God. Why? Because His love does not save you. Where are you told in the Scripture that love saves you? What we *are* told is,

For by grace you have been saved through faith, and that not of yourselves; it is the gift of God. (Ephesians 2:8)

God cannot love you into heaven. He had to do something about the sin first, because God is holy and cannot tolerate sin. Look with me at our most familiar verse, John 3:16, and let's take it apart to understand it better:

**For God so loved the world that He gave
His only begotten Son, that whoever
believes in Him should not perish but
have everlasting life.**

Does it say, "God so loved the world that He decided
to save it"? No. Does it imply that He broke out in
tears over us and sobbed, "Come on into heaven"?
No! God so loved the world that He gave His Son
to die. Because you and I are such terrible sinners, a holy God cannot let us in no matter how
much He loves us!

Now, I know that this presents a paradox. God
loves us, yet God hates us in our sin. Speaking in
human terms, God was confronted with a big problem: how to save sinners. (I've said this reverently,
because when you're dealing with an infinite God
you don't talk about problems, for He has none.)

The unchanging and righteous holiness of God
requires that "the soul who sins shall die" (Ezekiel
18:4). And yet God still says, "Yes, I have loved you
with an everlasting love; Therefore with lov-
ingkindness I have drawn you" (Jeremiah 31:3).
You see, the sin of man threw two attributes of God
out of adjustment—the holiness of God and the
love of God. Here's the sinner down here, and God
hates what he is doing. But God also loves His
creature. The holiness of God says the sinner must
be punished even though He loves him, so God
can't bring the sinner into heaven without doing

something about the sin. That, to us, presents a problem. God can't let down His standards.

In a Broadway play that was very popular years ago, an actor playing the part of the Lord God said to another actor playing the angel Gabriel, "Gabe, it ain't no picnic being God!" This business of saying He just loves everyone into heaven is the doctrine of the "Papa-hood" of God. As R. W. Dale, an English preacher and reformer, used to say, "It's the summer ocean of kindliness, never agitated by storms." But it is simply not true. He does not love anyone into heaven! It is much more difficult and much more drastic than that.

Our Lord said an awful and frightful thing while on the cross:

My God, My God, why have You forsaken Me? Why are You so far from helping Me, and from the words of My groaning? (Psalm 22:1)

Why? Will you tell me today why God forsook Him, the loveliest Person who ever walked this earth; the One of whom God had said, "This is My beloved Son, in whom I am well pleased" (Matthew 3:17)? Why does God's Son have to cry on the cross, "I'm forsaken"? You don't have to leave this psalm to find the answer: "But You are holy" (Psalm 22:3).

When the Son, the One who knew no sin, was made sin for us, my sin was put upon Him. And

God treated Him as He must treat every sinner who hangs on to sin—He forsook Jesus and allowed Him to die on a cross! God's holiness demanded that I be punished for my sin; His love for Me inspired Him to give His own Son to die in my place! I say to you that this makes God very wonderful and precious to me.

His Son left heaven's glory because He's a *holy* God. He could not lower the standards to get Vernon McGee into heaven, and so out of His great love He came down here, and He went to the cross, and He died on that cross for me. I know today that my God is not a lazy Buddha sitting with his legs crossed and arms folded, totally detached from the sin of man. The gods of the heathen never suffer, but our God is a God who has suffered for us.

In all their affliction He was afflicted, and the Angel of His Presence saved them; in His love and in His pity He redeemed them; and He bore them and carried them all the days of old. (Isaiah 63:9)

My God has come down into this world, and He took upon Himself my sin and your sin! Listen again to the psalmist:

Blessed be the Lord, who daily beareth our burden, even the God who is our salvation. (Psalm 68:19 ASV)

He goes with us and bears our burdens in the heat of the day. How wonderful that is!

After hearing the confessions of men who had come to him, Henry Drummond, who wrote *The Greatest Thing in the World* on the love of God, cried out in agony, "I'm sick of the sins of these men! How can God bear it?" Remember that Eliphaz felt the same way:

> **If God puts no trust in His saints, and the heavens are not pure in His sight, how much less man, who is abominable and filthy, who drinks iniquity like water!** (Job 15:15–16)

My friend, a holy God will not trifle with sin. He won't play with sin, and He won't let you play with sin either. He hates it! Do you think you're going to get by with it? If you do, then you must not believe that our God is a holy God. But He is a holy God, and you are not getting by with it—no matter how much He loves you. But, thank God, He made a way for us sinners to come and be saved from death.

> **This is the message which we have heard from Him and declare to you, that God is light and in Him is no darkness at all . . . But if we walk in the light as He is in the light, we have fellowship with one another,**

and the blood of Jesus Christ His Son cleanses [keeps on cleansing] **us from all sin. If we say that we have no sin, we deceive ourselves, and the truth is not in us.** (1 John 1:5, 7–8)

I'd like to close with an illustration. Years ago in the days of the sailing vessel, a captain was leaving England. His fourteen-year-old son begged to go with him, but the mother was reluctant to let him go. Finally, the father prevailed upon the mother, and the boy was allowed to go with his father. "But," his father warned him, "you will have to be a sailor and work on the ship right alongside me." While they were at sea, the boy was aloft and working in the rigging. All of a sudden a wind came up and whipped the arm around, leaving the boy caught and dangling there high above the ship. At any moment the boom would swing back around, and the boy would fall upon the deck and be killed. The father shouted to him to let go of the rigging and jump into the ocean. But the boy hesitated, afraid to jump into the water. The father quietly, slowly, drew out his revolver, pointed it at the boy and said, "Son, if you don't jump, I'll shoot." The boy knew his dad and knew that he meant business. So, more afraid of the gun, the boy made a leap into the water. No sooner had he hit the water than his father's great, strong arms were under him, bringing him safely to the surface and back on deck.

May I say to you, beloved, the holiness of God is a gun pointing at you. It's loaded with the Law, the Ten Commandments. You think you can break them and get by with it, but you can't. God says you have to choose. You can jump into the ocean of His love, and you'll find there a Savior with nail-pierced hands who died in your place because you are a hopeless sinner! If you don't jump you will be lost forever in a Christless eternity. His holiness says that you must die in your sins. But He will lift you up and save you because He loves you and wants to be with you. That's the way a holy God saves sinners.

CHAPTER 5

DOES GOD EVER CHANGE HIS MIND?

Does God ever change His mind? In view of the fact that we have to begin somewhere, let's begin with the first chapter of James, verse 17:

> **Every good gift and every perfect gift is from above, and comes down from the Father of lights, with whom there is no variation or shadow of turning.**

God never changes. He's exempt from any modification whatsoever. Actually, there is no change possible within Him. It is impossible for there to be a deviation by one hair's breadth; this, my beloved, is called the immutability of God. God is immutable—He never changes His mind. He can't change for better because God is absolute perfection. He fills the universe and there can be no variation in that because He simply cannot be more than He already is. And then He could not be worse nor could He be less. If He were, He would not be God because it's inconsistent with perfection to have change. Therefore, in the person of God there is no extension nor is there any declension whatsoever.

One summer I went back to where I grew up and where I was educated, and I didn't recognize the place. Only here and there did I see things that brought back memories from my youth. There had been such a change—nothing in the entire area even looked the same! It was altogether different. But it is a physical place, and it changed because time, people, weather, and technology have a tendency to change things.

However, the minute we move out of the realm of creation and begin talking about God, there's no *reason* for God to change. He does not have some new information today that He did not already have yesterday. Nothing unexpected has come His way today that would cause Him to alter His plan. There is nothing appearing on the horizon that God did not foresee. He doesn't read the morning paper to find out what happened last night—in fact, it wouldn't have happened if He had not permitted it. My friends, He knows everything from the very beginning to the very end.

May I say to you, the Scripture has a great deal to say on this subject. I'd like to call your attention to several passages. In Job 23:13–14, Job makes this observation about God:

> **But He is unique, and who can make Him change? And whatever His soul desires, that He does. For He performs what is appointed for me, and many such things are with Him.**

Also, Isaiah had something to say along this line. God, speaking through him, said,

> **Remember the former things of old, for I am God, and there is no other; I am God, and there is none like Me, declaring the end from the beginning, and from ancient times things that are not yet done, saying, "My counsel shall stand, and I will do all My pleasure."** (Isaiah 46:9–10)

And the psalmist said in Psalm 102:27, "But You are the same, and Your years will have no end."

In other words, God does not learn by experience. He does not need experience and He has not come to the place where He is today because of the experience of the past. There's no danger of Him losing His position, and nothing has ever happened that has surprised Him. He never uses the trial-and-error method. Colleges today could not teach Him anything—although I think the colleges believe they could! The fact of the matter is that He could teach some of them a great deal. May I say to you, God knew all things from the very beginning and, therefore, there has been no reason for Him to change anything in His plan or in His program.

I was very much interested in an engineering magazine that was sent to me once, although I could understand only about half of what I read. But I did understand this: *Changing economic orders present new problems that demand new methods and new solutions.* Well, for mankind that certainly is obvious. We're living today in a world that has changed so much that we must have new solutions to the problems that continually come up. But God doesn't need solutions, my beloved. All that seems new and overwhelming or amazing to us is old hat to Him today. The introduction of a nuclear age did not present Him with some intricate or complex problem. He's moving right along with His own very complex and intricate program, and He knows every detail of it.

Now, I want to clarify what has been said because some might get the wrong impression concerning God. To say that God is immutable and that He does not change His mind does not mean that God is like a stone fence. It does not mean that He is adamant or that there is a stereotyped sameness about Him. It doesn't mean that there is no flexibility and it certainly doesn't mean a monotonous status quo. *Immutability* is not *immobility*. If it were, it would be the same as the Greek style of worship. They worshiped the three fates called the Moirai: Clotho spun the cord of time, Lachesis determined how long it was going to be, and Atropos cut the string—she had the scissors. There was absolutely nothing a person could do about it. The Greeks thought of that as fatalism. But when it comes to the character of God, we are not dealing with fatalism at all.

Let us look at three classic illustrations given in the Scriptures of when God *did* change His mind, or so it seems to us. What does it mean when on three occasions we read that God repented? The first reference I want us to consider is in the Book of Genesis:

> **And the LORD was sorry** [repented] **that He had made man on the earth, and He was grieved in His heart.** (Genesis 6:6)

As I noted before, the Bible often uses anthropomorphic terms to speak of God so that you and I can understand Him. For instance, it speaks of His eyes, "The eyes of the LORD run to and fro throughout the whole earth" (2 Chronicles 16:9). It also speaks of the ears of God, the arm of God, and the hand of God. But these are anthropomorphic terms, for He says this: "He who planted the ear, shall He not hear? He who formed the eye, shall He not see?" (Psalm 94:9). I'll be very honest with you, I cannot understand how God can hear unless He's got an ear. So if you say that He has an ear I get the point—it gets through to me that God hears. But, friends, God doesn't really have an ear in the physical form we are familiar with. I don't know *how* God can hear without an ear, but He does. And I have a notion you feel the same as I do—the use of an anthropomorphic term is the only way we can understand certain concepts.

There's another device used in Scripture known as anthropopathism. That's a big word that simply means to give human feelings to something that isn't human—in this case, God. The Bible says, for instance, "He who sits in the heavens shall laugh" (Psalm 2:4). It's an emotional term to say that God laughs. I don't know how anyone can laugh without a mouth, but it says here that God laughs. Then, too, the Bible says that God weeps, also that God is grieved, and it plainly states that God repents. These terms refer to us humans psychologically, and they are used in relation to God so that we can understand something about Him.

After God had created man we come to the time of the Flood and Scripture says, "And the LORD was sorry [repented] that He had made man." *Repent* means to change your mind. Had God changed His mind about man?

The King James Version uses the word *repented*, and actually the word here for *repented* is different from our word for repentance (I looked this up in my Greek Septuagint translation which, in my opinion, is probably more accurate than the original Hebrew at this point). It's not *metanoia* meaning "to change your mind." Actually the word used here expresses a note of grief. I think we need to understand this—it's important to try to discover the exact meaning of words. God tells us here, "And it repented the LORD that he had made man on the earth" (Genesis 6:6 KJV). "*It* repented the Lord." What is meant by "it"? What was it that caused our Lord to repent? Well, let's keep reading:

Then the LORD saw that the wickedness of man was great in the earth, and that every intent of the thoughts of his heart was only evil continually. (Genesis 6:5)

This is what grieved God—the wickedness and the sin of man.

God created Adam and Eve and put them in the Garden of Eden. I believe He created them for several reasons and that one of them was for fellowship. And since they were created as free moral agents there must be a choice somewhere in that garden to test their obedience to their Creator. That choice was the tree of the knowledge of good and evil. At that time God said if they ate of that tree they were going to die. May I say to you that Adam and Eve ate of the tree and *did* die. Nowhere along here does God change His mind. What God said at the beginning was, "In the day that you eat of it you shall surely die" (Genesis 2:17). And when Adam and Eve ate that fruit, God did exactly what He said He would do. He didn't change His mind; He kept His Word.

If we go into sin, our Lord tells us the same thing He told Cain, "Oh, sin lies at your door. But you can come to Me and I'll extend mercy to you" (see Genesis 4:7). And God patiently—over a period of at least nine hundred years—watched the human family multiply upon the earth, and He was grieved because so few were coming to Him for mercy. Eventually there was only one righteous man and God said, "I've got to stop this while I have one man. I cannot let this go to the next generation, otherwise Ham, Shem, and Japheth will not serve Me. So for the sake of the race, I must intervene." (see Genesis 6:9–13). God did save Noah and his household, and for one hundred and twenty years Noah was faithful in preaching. God didn't change His mind. God always punishes sin, and God will always save the sinner who comes to Him. Anybody could have gotten on that ark if he had only believed God.

The people of Noah's day were like a lot of folk today who just don't believe God. God did not change His mind. Then who changed? Mankind changed. The people whom God created to walk with Him turned away from Him in rebellion. The natural man is an enemy of God. Paul says that this old nature, the flesh, is at enmity with God—that is, actually the enemy of God—and is going its own way into sin. God had to destroy man from off the earth, and the reason was because God never changes. Mankind radically changed and became corrupt, and God treated them as He must always treat lost sinners going on in rebellion. He had to judge the earth.

What repented God and grieved Him was man's changed action, because God loved and wanted man for His own. He did not want to destroy him, for "it is not the will of your Father who is in heaven that one of these little ones should perish" (Matthew 18:14). God hasn't created us to be lost—He wants to save us. God has never changed from that position.

Now alongside Genesis 6, we need to consider this statement:

> **God is not a man, that He should lie, nor a son of man, that He should repent. Has He said, and will He not do? Or has He spoken, and will He not make it good?** (Numbers 23:19)

My friend, you can depend on God doing exactly what He says He will do. Does that mean that what we see in Genesis is God's sorrow? Yes, because He has not changed His mind.

> **So the LORD said, "I will destroy man whom I have created from the face of the earth, both man and beast, creeping thing and birds of the air, for I am sorry that I have made them."** (Genesis 6:7)

In effect, God is saying, "This was not My original purpose for man. I created man to live forever, and I have not changed. I told Adam at the very beginning that in the day he ate thereof he would die. And sin was at the door of any one of Adam's progeny after that. If they continued on in sin I'd have to drive them out from My presence."

So here is man multiplying on the face of the earth yet living in rebellion against God. Finally there is only one man left and God intervenes graciously for the sake of future generations so that He might save the human family.

Let's move on to the second classic incident in the Word of God where it appears to us that God changed His mind. In 1 Samuel 15:11, God is speaking:

> **"I greatly regret that I have set up Saul as king, for he has turned back from following Me, and has not performed My commandments." And it grieved Samuel, and he cried out to the LORD all night.**

How Samuel loved Saul! The fact of the matter is that Samuel was never really sold on David, but he was sold on Saul. So when God came to him and told him, "I have rejected Saul," it broke Samuel's heart. He spent all night weeping before the Lord, pleading with God to let Saul continue on as king. But instead, God commanded Samuel to go out and confront Saul on His behalf.

Actually it was the people who wanted Saul in the first place. In fact, they demanded him and God acceded to their demands. This man Saul looked like a king. Scripture makes it very clear that he stood head and shoulders above everyone else. Physically he was a giant; spiritually and in things pertaining to God, he was a midget.

Now, this man was commanded by God to use extreme surgery on the Amalekites in order to eliminate the growing cancer in the land. But like a great many people today (even preachers), Saul soft-pedaled God's message and spared the Amalekites' king and their best cattle. The reason God wanted all the flocks and herds and all the booty destroyed was that He never wanted His people to get interested in warfare just for the sake of getting rich or bettering their circumstances with things that belonged to somebody else. Another reason was that these pagan people were thoroughly infected with venereal diseases, so much so that in Joshua's day God hadn't let His people touch anything in the city of Jericho.

But Saul decided to save some of the sheep and oxen and, as usual, came up with a pious reason for his disobedience. I want you to notice the thing that he used as an excuse, because it's a lame excuse. He said, "I'll save the cattle and we'll use the best of them for a sacrifice to God." Now isn't that a pathetic cover-up?

Do you think God saw through it? He said to Samuel, "You go over and confront Saul. He has disobeyed Me."

> **So when Samuel rose early in the morning to meet Saul, it was told Samuel, saying, "Saul went to Carmel, and indeed, he set up a monument for himself; and he has gone on around, passed by, and gone down to Gilgal." (1 Samuel 15:12)**

Saul had moved on out and Samuel had to chase after him. Notice Saul's false piety when Samuel finally found him:

> **Then Samuel went to Saul, and Saul said to him, "Blessed are you of the LORD! I have performed the commandment of the LORD." (1 Samuel 15:13)**

But God had just told Samuel that Saul had *not* performed His commandment. Saul, you see, was like a great many folk today who partially do what God asks them to do but won't go all out, yet they still think they are in fellowship with God.

Samuel then spoke for the Lord and said, "If you have obeyed God, why do I hear cows lowing in the distance? And what then is this bleating of sheep in my ears?" (see 1 Samuel 15:14).

"Oh," Saul said, "*they* have brought them from the Amalekites, haven't you heard? *I* didn't do it, the people did it." He blamed the people! "For the people spared the best of the sheep and the oxen, to sacrifice to the LORD *your* God [why isn't He Saul's God?]; and the rest we have utterly destroyed" (1 Samuel 15:15, emphasis mine).

An obvious question arises here: Was Saul saved or not? I do not intend to answer that other than to express my own conviction. I do not believe Saul was a true believer. I think he was absolutely a lost man. He was one of the forerunners of the Antichrist who is to come. The Antichrist will be religious, as you know, and quite similar to this man Saul who was outwardly very religious.

At this juncture Saul is told by Samuel, "God has rejected you from being king." Now if Saul were honest and genuine he would have put on sackcloth and ashes. But did he? No, he wanted to keep up a front. He didn't want the people to know just how bad he really was. So he said to Samuel,

"Now therefore, please pardon my sin, and return with me, that I may worship

the LORD." But Samuel said to Saul, "I will
not return with you, for you have rejected
the word of the LORD, and the LORD has
rejected you from being king over Israel."
(1 Samuel 15:25–26)

The man who should have been in sackcloth and
ashes wanted to put on his royal robes and go out
and put up a front before God and the people—
that was Saul. He was not genuine at all. He was
a phony, as phony as a three-dollar bill.

I wonder today how many of us in the church
are keeping up a front before the rest of the congregation while inside is a festering sore of sin
and rebellion against God. Yet, oh, how pious we
can be on Sunday! What a front we can put up
before everyone else when we ourselves should
be flat on our faces before God, asking for for-
giveness.

This man Saul went on with his rebellion.
Listen to Saul's so-called repentance,

Then he said, "I have sinned; yet honor
me now, please, before the elders of my
people and before Israel, and return with
me, that I may worship the LORD your
God." (1 Samuel 15:30)

Not *my* God, but *your* God. He's still trying to
keep up a front.

> So Samuel said to him, "The LORD has
> torn the kingdom of Israel from you
> today, and has given it to a neighbor of
> yours, who is better than you. And also
> the Strength of Israel will not lie nor
> relent. For He is not a man, that He
> should relent." (1 Samuel 15:28–29)

Did God repent? Did He change His mind
about making Saul the king? No, friends, God has
not changed. God will not accept a phony to continue as king over His people. Notice His stinging
rebuke:

> Behold, to obey is better than sacrifice,
> and to heed than the fat of rams. (1 Samuel
> 15:22)

Oh, if you would only *obey* God, He would bless
you! And because you have not obeyed Him, He
will judge you. And why? For the simple reason
that God never changes.

But He *is* grieved over you. He *will* weep for
you. You can break His heart, but you can't
change Him. May I say that the immutability of
God is the terror of the wicked today. Every
wicked person would like to believe two things:
one, that there is no God or that somehow He's
going to break down in tears at the last moment
and not be able to go through with His pronounced

judgment; and, *two,* that hell is no reality and sin will not be punished. The wicked would like to believe that, but, my friend, God does not change.

There was a lady in a cult who once came down to the front after a church service to speak to me. She said, "Dr. McGee, I don't like the way you preach. You preach the judgment of God for sin, but that's the Old Testament. The Old Testament God is a God of judgment, a God of wrath. Now, in the New Testament He is a God of love."

Well, I talked with her for a few moments and then I said, "Look, I want you to consider something. You say that the God of the New Testament is a God of love, the God of the Old Testament is a God of wrath. But God destroyed Sodom and Gomorrah."

She said, "Yeah, that's what I was just telling you—He's a God of wrath."

I said, "Yes, but in the Old Testament He saved the city of Nineveh, the most wicked pagan city of the day. When you get to the New Testament, you see the Lord Jesus and you say that He's gentle and that He is love. I agree with you. I see Him sitting yonder on the Mount of Olives, looking over Jerusalem, and I see Him weeping. Why is He weeping?" And I read to her the following verses:

O Jerusalem, Jerusalem, the one who kills the prophets and stones those who are sent to her! How often I wanted to

gather your children together, as a hen
gathers her chicks under her wings, but
you were not willing! See! Your house is
left to you desolate. . . . Assuredly, I say to
you, not one stone shall be left here upon
another, that shall not be thrown down.
(Matthew 23:37–38; 24:2)

Then I said, "Have you ever read about the
destruction of Jerusalem in A.D. 70 when mothers
ate their own children?"

"No, I haven't, and I don't want to read it."

"You just don't want to face the truth," I said.
"God has not changed. The One in the Old
Testament who destroyed Sodom and Gomorrah
is the One in the New Testament who destroyed
Jerusalem. And the One in the Old Testament
who saved Nineveh is the One today who will
save any person who comes to Him."

The reason is that God never changes. In fact,
God has *never* changed—that's the terror of the
wicked.

Let's look at John 3:16. We are always empha-
sizing God's love for the world. Why? Because "He
gave His only begotten Son [that's wonderful, we
love it], that whoever believes in Him [that's
great, oh, we love it] should not perish [we don't
like to think about that]." But the reason God
gave His Son was because mankind was perish-
ing, and without Christ man *will* perish. Why?

Because God never changes His mind. Do you think that somehow you can come up on the blind side of God and use some sort of salesmanship, maybe something you read in the book *How to Make Friends and Influence People*? Do you think you're going to talk Him out of judging your sin? I think not. God never changes.

I come now to the last example. This is a very familiar incident, one that is probably well known to you. It's the story of Jonah's experience with the people of Nineveh. There's something very interesting said here about Nineveh:

> **Then God saw their works, that they turned from their evil way; and God relented from the disaster that He had said He would bring upon them, and He did not do it.** (Jonah 3:10)

I have a notion that somebody is sure now that I've been wrong all along, because it says specifically that God changed—He was going to destroy Nineveh but He did not do it. It's true—He did say He was going to destroy it. That was the message Jonah brought into the city:

> **And Jonah began to enter the city on the first day's walk. Then he cried out and said, "Yet forty days, and Nineveh shall be overthrown!"** (Jonah 3:4)

Now why did God send Jonah to Nineveh in the first place? Well, God asked Jonah, "And should I not pity Nineveh, that great city . . .?" (Jonah 4:11). The reason God sent Jonah to Nineveh was that He wanted to spare Nineveh. He wanted to save the people in that wicked city, and so He sent this man Jonah down there. At the very beginning God said, "Arise, go to Nineveh, that great city, and cry out against it; for their wickedness has come up before Me" (Jonah 1:2).

So who was it that changed? Did God change? No, my beloved. There is an axiom that God will always judge sin. God said to Nineveh, "If you continue on in your sin I will destroy you," but He wanted to spare Nineveh. And the people of Nineveh—from the king's throne room all the way down into the slums—went into sackcloth and ashes and cried mightily unto God for deliverance. And do you know what God did? God heard them and God saved them! Do you know why He saved them? Because God never changes. When the people of a wicked city humble themselves and turn to God, God will spare them—always. He has never changed. It may have looked as if He changed because He said He was going to destroy the city, but He also said that He would save. And Nineveh turned to God, so God saved Nineveh.

To the casual reader it seems that God had repented and changed His mind; but if Nineveh had continued on in sin, would God have destroyed the city? Well, if you want the answer to that question, turn to the prophecy of Nahum a hundred years later when God *did* destroy the city of Nineveh, for at that time they did not turn to God. God would have destroyed Nineveh in Jonah's day, but the reason He didn't is because Nineveh changed, and when a city or an individual changes and turns to God, God will save because *He never changes.*

Let me illustrate this. Imagine a man riding a bicycle into a strong wind. It's holding him back and keeping him from reaching his goal. The man gets very tired, so he turns around and starts riding in the opposite direction. The wind that was holding him back now pushes him along. Has the wind changed? No, the wind hasn't changed, it's blowing in the same direction. It looks as though the wind has changed because it's having the opposite effect on the man, but the man is the one who changed. When a person lives in rebellion against God but then turns back to Him, God will always save. God is the One who never changes. I said previously that the immutability of God is the terror of the wicked, but, my friend, the same immutability of God is also the comfort of the child of God.

I think one of the loveliest things said about old Jacob was that "he came to Bethel." If you read Jacob's story very carefully you will see that he had a limited view of God at first. Jacob was surprised to find God at Bethel. Actually, when he ran away from home and away from Esau, he thought he had gotten rid of God, too. But that night God spoke to him through a dream and Jacob said, "I'll call this place Bethel because God is in this place." (see Genesis 28:19). Bethel means "house of God," and God dealt with Jacob there and even made a covenant with him.

Then Jacob traveled on to Haran. A quarter of a century went by, and for Jacob it was a checkered sort of experience. On the one hand he discovered and enjoyed the great love of his life— beautiful Rachel. But on the other hand it was terrible. Uncle Laban was used by God to take Jacob to the woodshed. He suffered injustice and trickery time and time again. In reading the story, we might suppose that God was through with Jacob, that He had abandoned this wayward man. But when Jacob came back into his homeland, notice God's gracious response—this is so wonderful:

Then God said to Jacob, "Arise, go up to Bethel and dwell there; and make an altar there to God, who appeared to you when you fled from the face of Esau your brother." (Genesis 35:1)

In essence, God is telling him, "Go back to Bethel, Jacob. I haven't changed, I'm right here. I'm right here to meet you and to greet you and to bless you." How wonderful God is!

Our Lord told the story about a father waiting for a son who had run away. The father never changed—he loved the boy. One day the boy changed and came home. And when he did, the father ran to meet him. An old Scottish commentator said that's the only time God ever gets in a hurry. He runs to meet His wayward child because God never changes.

> It fortifies my soul to know
> That, though I perish, Truth is so:
> That, howsoe'er I stray and range,
> Whate'er I do, Thou dost not change.
> I steadier step when I recall
> That, if I slip, Thou dost not fall.
> —Arthur Hugh Clough[1]

I have a God today on whom I can depend. He can't depend on me, but I can depend on Him—He will never change. Our Lord is the same yesterday, today, and forever. In fact, He is the same today as He was the day He hung on the cross. He didn't work Himself up into some great emotional pitch just to die on the cross. When He died on that cross it was the expression of the same love He has for you today. He will never turn against the one who turns to Him—never.

Jesus Christ is the same yesterday, today, and forever. (Hebrews 13:8)

God's message through Malachi to His people is,

For I am the LORD, I do not change; therefore you are not consumed, O sons of Jacob. (Malachi 3:6)

My friend, He knew the day He saved you that you were going to fall, so He made arrangements for you. He says to you and to me, "If we confess our sins, He is faithful and just to forgive us our sins and to cleanse us from all unrighteousness" (1 John 1:9). What a comfort it is to know that He will never change His mind about that!

CHAPTER 6

HOW CAN GOD EXIST IN THREE PERSONS?

The great English poet Samuel Taylor Coleridge, in a conversation with Robert Browning remarked, "I read all your poetry, but nine-tenths of it I do not understand." Robert Browning answered him by saying, "Sir, a person of your caliber ought to be satisfied if he understands one-tenth."

Well, I have spent more than a quarter of a century in serious study of the Word of God, and I confess to my appalling ignorance in certain areas, especially in the subject of the Trinity. If you could have met me the year I graduated from seminary, you would have heard me give absolute answers to all your questions. But I am unable to do that today. In fact, I would be content if I understood one-tenth of the great truth concerning our triune God.

I assure you that with all my heart I believe in the Trinity. I revel and rejoice in it, believing that it is not only a great truth but also one of the unique truths of the Christian faith. But I confess that I find it to be an enigmatic mystery, an inscrutable riddle. I find that it is complicated, complex, bewildering, and impossible to explain. Why?

One reason is that the Trinity is not geared to this mechanical age. Tensions and pressures hurry us through life. A cartoonist has pictured a man sitting in a one-counter restaurant, giving his order to the waitress. He is saying, "I have to be at work in twenty-three minutes. I want one-minute oatmeal, three-minute eggs, two-minute bacon, forty-five second toast, and instant coffee." An age that goes at a pace like that is not an age that will know very much about the Trinity. The Trinity cannot be explained in just a few moments. It is doubtful if it can ever be satisfactorily explained, yet we need to study it carefully.

For several hundred years after the apostles lived, the Trinity was a most important subject to intelligent men. Men like Irenaeus, Tertullian, Athanasius, Origen, and Augustine gave themselves to the study of this great doctrine. It was the all-engrossing topic that men of keen intellect spent their time pondering. As a result, the doctrine of the Trinity broadly affected European life for centuries. From the day of the apostles until about the seventh century it was very important to multitudes of people. The economic, political, and social spheres were all essentially influenced by this truth. Rulers reigned, armies marched, and diplomats convened as this truth helped shape the destiny of Europe.

All so-called theological liberalism is basically off at this point. Behind the denial of the deity of Christ is the denial of the Trinity. This denial came into America by way of New England through the Congregational churches, which eventually became largely Unitarian churches. There is an ancient adage that warns that those who try to understand the Trinity lose their minds and those who deny the Trinity lose their souls. We are caught in that kind of dilemma. Although we shall not be able to understand it fully, or perhaps not even satisfactorily, we shall at least stand on the fringe of this great truth and worship.

We will look at the *definition* of the Trinity, then the *declaration* in Scripture of the Trinity, and finally *illustrations* of the Trinity from nature.

The Trinity Defined

First is the definition of the Trinity. What do we mean by "the Trinity"? We mean three Persons in the Godhead. There are two extremes that we need to avoid. They are like Scylla on one hand and Charybdis on the other (two equally dangerous monsters), and we need to sail our little bark between them.

The initial danger, when speaking of the Trinity, is to have in mind three gods. That is a false concept. Then there is the other extreme of holding that the one God has expressed Himself in three different ways, which is also false. This error, known as modal-Trinitarianism, was thoroughly answered by some of the giants of the faith whom we have already named.

I turn now to what I believe is the best statement made on this subject. It is in the Westminster Confession of Faith. The question is asked: "How many persons are there in the Godhead?" The answer is: "There are three persons in the Godhead: the Father, the Son, and the Holy Ghost; and these three are one God, the same in substance, equal in power and glory." That definition is the finest to be found.

Now notice that three Persons constitute one Being, one God. Peter, James, and John are not a trinity. They are three persons, but they are not the same, they are not equal. There are three chairs before me. They look alike and probably are constructed of the same material—possibly of the same tree—yet they are not a trinity.

God is one Being, and yet He is three Persons. However, these three have one nature. For instance, a great many like to make a distinction by saying that God is holy, Christ is love, and the

Holy Spirit is infinite. Such is a false distinction, for God is holy, Christ is holy, and the Holy Spirit is holy; God is love (that is one of His definitions), Christ is love, and the Holy Spirit is love; God is infinite, Christ is infinite, and the Holy Spirit is infinite.

The three Persons are also the same in their attributes, in their will, and in their purpose. What one wills, all will. When the Lord Jesus came to earth He made this very clear. He said, "I have come to do My Father's will." (see John 14 and 15). What He had come to do was in harmony with the Father, for all three were in agreement. He came to do the Father's will; He came to do His own will, which was evident; and He came to do the will of the Holy Spirit—He was led and guided by the Spirit of God.

Each one is God. Christ did not become a Son over time. He was always the only begotten Son of God. You see, God is called the everlasting Father, and you cannot have an everlasting Father unless you have an everlasting Son. There never was a time when Christ *became* the Son— He eternally occupies that position in the Trinity.

Another false way of stating it is to say that God is the Father, Christ is the Son, and the Holy Spirit is sort of like the Grandson. There was never a time when God was not the Father, there was never a time when Christ was not the Son, and there was never a time when the Holy Spirit was not the Holy Spirit. There are some who will say that because the Lord Jesus Christ came to this earth as a man, He is not equal with the Father. This is also wrong, for He said, "The Father and I are one" (John 10:30).

They have the same nature. There are not three gods and they are never opposed to one another. What one does all of them do. The clarity of this fact can do nothing but make us stand on the fringe and know that we are in the presence of the Infinite.

The Trinity Declared by Scripture

We come now to the declaration in Scripture of the Trinity. I hasten to say that the word *trinity* is not used in Scripture. But neither is the word *atonement* used in the New Testament (the word incorrectly translated as *atonement* in Romans 5:11 [KJV] is actually *reconciliation*). But although the word does not appear in the New Testament, it certainly teaches what the Old Testament presents as the Atonement. It is not necessary to have the word, because that which the word signifies is taught in the New Testament Scripture. Since the word *trinity* does not appear in Scripture, does the Bible actually teach the doctrine of the Trinity? If it does not, we can dismiss the subject and forget about it. But if the Word of God does teach the Trinity, then we should believe it.

Someone may say, "Before I believe it I want to understand it." If truth is only that which we understand, may I say that there is not much that is true today, for we are quite limited in our understanding. On such a basis, trigonometry and organic chemistry are not true because I don't understand them. In college I had no desire to understand them, and today I still have no desire to understand these two subjects. Yet I do not take the awkward and ignorant position that they are not true subjects—they are. Thankfully, truth is not limited to my little mind or to your little mind. There are those today who, because they cannot understand the Trinity, want to dismiss it. However, the real question is: *Does the Word of God teach the Trinity?*

The Trinity in the Old Testament

I turn back now to the Old Testament because it clearly teaches the Trinity. The verse of Scripture that is probably the greatest doctrinal statement in the Old Testament is found in the Book of Deuteronomy:

> **Hear, O Israel: The LORD our God, the LORD is one!** (Deuteronomy 6:4)

If you want a literal translation, it is, "Hear, O Israel: the LORD our plural God is one God!" The word *one* is *echad*, the same word used back in

Genesis 2:24 when God said, concerning Adam and Eve, "And they shall become one flesh." Two persons become one. In that mysterious relationship of marriage, two people are made one, which is evident always in the child. They shall be one flesh, though two—two in one. This is the word used in Deuteronomy 6:4 (my paraphrase), "Hear, O Israel: Elohim—our plural God, our Trinity, tripersonality—is one God!" The mysterious One, like Adam and Eve made one flesh, is three Persons in one. That is a wonderful truth and unfathomable by human reason.

Scripture, you see, teaches the Trinity. The Old Testament repeatedly declares the plurality of God. If you go back to the first chapter of Genesis, you will see this again:

> **Then God said, "Let Us make man in Our image, according to Our likeness; let them have dominion over the fish of the sea, over the birds of the air, and over the cattle, over all the earth and over every creeping thing that creeps on the earth." So God created man in His own image; in the image of God He created him; male and female He created them.** (Genesis 1:26–27)

Notice that God said, "Let *Us* make man in *Our* image." It is plural. Then in the eleventh chapter of Genesis, at the Tower of Babel, God said:

"Come, let Us go down and there confuse their language, that they may not understand one another's speech." So the Lord scattered them abroad from there over the face of all the earth, and they ceased building the city. (vv. 7–8)

We see here that the Lord scattered them, but He said, "Let *Us* go down." The Trinity came down, but He is still one God.

Moving on in the Old Testament we find that Isaiah said:

Also I heard the voice of the Lord, saying: "Whom shall I send, and who will go for Us?" Then I said, "Here am I! Send me." (Isaiah 6:8)

Before this, Isaiah had gone into the temple and heard the seraphim saying, "Holy, holy, holy"— not twice, not four times, but three times. It was a praise to the triune God. Holy is the Father, holy is the Son, and holy is the Spirit.

In Ecclesiastes we read the familiar words, "Remember now your Creator in the days of your youth" (12:1). The word *Creator* is *Boreacho*, which means "Creators," plural. "Remember now thy Creators, thy Trinity"—for the Trinity was involved in creation, as you well know. We are told that God the Father was the Creator, "In the beginning God created . . ." Both the Gospel of John (1:3) and the Epistle to the Colossians (1:16) tell us that the Lord Jesus Christ was the Creator. Also we are told that the Holy Spirit of God was the Creator: "The Spirit of God was hovering over the face of the waters" (Genesis 1:2). Thus it is evident that the Trinity was involved in creation just as the Trinity is involved in redemption.

In the Old Testament, Israel witnessed to a polytheistic world—a civilization with many gods—concerning the unity of the Godhead. That was the mission of Israel in the ancient world. The mission of the church in this day is to a world not given to polytheism (the worship of many gods), but to atheism (the worship of no god). To our godless civilization we are to witness to the Trinity. For that reason the Unitarian doctrine that God exists only in one person is a damnable heresy that has injured America more than any other thing. It is what has softened and weakened this great country of ours.

The Trinity in the New Testament

The Trinity is an explicit and peculiar doctrine of the New Testament.

The record in the Gospels of the baptism of the Lord Jesus Christ graphically presents the Trinity. At the time the Lord Jesus was baptized He saw the Holy Spirit as a dove coming upon

Him, and the voice of the Father from heaven spoke saying, "This is My beloved Son, in whom I am well pleased" (Matthew 3:17). The Trinity—the Father, Son, and Holy Spirit—is clearly brought before us on this occasion.

Again, in the baptismal formula that Jesus gave to His apostles when He sent them out, He said, ". . . baptizing them in the name of the Father and of the Son and of the Holy Spirit" (Matthew 28:19).

Paul, in his apostolic benediction, includes the three persons of the Godhead:

> **The grace of the *Lord Jesus Christ,* and the love of *God,* and the communion of the *Holy Spirit* be with you all. Amen.** (2 Corinthians 13:14, emphasis mine)

The Lord Jesus even taught His disciples the doctrine of the Trinity:

> **And *I* will pray the *Father,* and He will give you another *Helper* [like I am, on the same par with Me], that He may abide with you forever."** (John 14:16, emphasis mine)

The New Testament abounds with the teaching of the Trinity, for it repeatedly names the three persons of the Godhead. We have a *Father* who is God:

To all who are in Rome, beloved of God, called to be saints: Grace to you and peace from *God our Father* and the Lord Jesus Christ. (Romans 1:7, emphasis mine)

We have presented to us in the New Testament a *Son* who is God:

But to the *Son* He says: "Your throne, *O God,* is forever and ever; a scepter of righteousness is the scepter of Your kingdom." (Hebrews 1:8, emphasis mine)

Also the *Holy Spirit* is presented as God. At the incident involving Ananias and Sapphira, Peter said:

Ananias, why has Satan filled your heart to lie to the *Holy Spirit* and keep back part of the price of the land for yourself? While it remained, was it not your own? And after it was sold, was it not in your own control? Why have you conceived this thing in your heart? You have not lied to men but to *God.* (Acts 5:3–4, emphasis mine)

Peter is saying here, "You have lied to the Holy Spirit, and when you have lied to the Holy Spirit you have lied to God." The Holy Spirit is God.

The Trinity Illustrated by Nature

We come now to our third point, illustrations from nature of the Trinity.

I repeat the question: Is it possible to understand the Trinity? If the answer must be either yes or no, it has to be an emphatic *no*. The centuries have revealed that the intellect of the genius, the perspicuity of the philosopher, the comprehension of the scientist, and the lucidity of the orator have not been enough to make clear the Trinity. The reason is this: There are no perfect examples that can be used, because it is impossible to demonstrate the infinite God by finite creation. We cannot employ the creation to illustrate adequately the Creator in His person. Now it is true that the *love* of God can be illustrated by human love. You can take that feeling of love and translate it into human terminology. You see a mother bending over the crib of her little baby and somehow it illustrates something of God's great pulsating love for us. But in nature you find no such illustration for the Trinity. Yet I shall dare to pull in several illustrations from nature that may be somewhat helpful.

Man Is a Trinity
First of all, I want to look at man himself.

Now may the God of peace Himself sanc-
tify you completely [your total personality];
and may your whole spirit, soul, and body
be preserved blameless at the coming of
our Lord Jesus Christ. (1 Thessalonians
5:23)

Man was created in the image of God, and so
man is a trinity—body, soul, and spirit. Believe
me, if we could understand human nature, we
would have a better understanding of God. But
we do not understand even ourselves. Psychology
has wrestled with this. When psychology began,
it dealt only with the spirit or the soul. Then it
found it was on the wrong track, and it swung
over to the opposite extreme, as in my day when
the psychology studied in college was behaviorism.
It taught that we are only physical, that we are
like a series of push buttons. You push *this* button
and you get *that* reaction. The difficulty is that
you push a certain button on one fellow and get a
certain reaction, but you push the same button on
another fellow and you get a different reaction.
Since that theory did not work, psychology
changed its mind again and said that we are more
than body and more than just spirit. Psychology
now admits that man is a threefold being: Man is
sarcous, man is psychic, and man is pneumatic.
In other words, there is the body, there is the psy-
chological part, and there is the spiritual part. We

are more than body; we are more than just mind; we are more than spirit.

By the way, I am thankful we are more than spirit. What a relief it was to me when I found out that I was not going to be an angel. When I was a little fellow in Sunday school they taught us to sing, "I want to be an angel, and with the angels sing." Well, *I* never wanted to be an angel because I thought angels flitted around without bodies, which never suited me at all. I am thankful that throughout eternity we are to have bodies. We have been created a trinity—body, soul, and spirit.

When we say that we do not understand the Trinity, we must confess that neither do we understand ourselves. When we better understand man, we shall understand something of the Trinity that is God.

Music Is a Trinity

Let me move now into another realm of nature—the field of music. I am told that in music there are seven tones on the major scale but that there are only three structural tones. These are the principal chords: the tonic, the subdominant, and the dominant. These are the three major tones, and out of them comes all of our music. You cannot have harmony without these three.

There is the harmony of heaven. The Word of God speaks of it before man was created "when the morning stars sang together, and all the sons of God shouted for joy" (Job 38:7). This heavenly music was based on a trinity—you cannot have harmony without it.

Thus in the realm of music you have the three that make one, and the one is harmony.

Water Is a Trinity

Let us move further into nature and consider water. Water is used in the Scriptures as a picture of God—He is spoken of as water. Listen to the psalm that is David's heart cry:

> **As the deer pants for the water brooks, so pants my soul for You, O God. My soul thirsts for God, for the living God.** (Psalm 42:1–2)

David is saying here, "What the water brook is to a little animal, that is what God is to me."

Then notice another psalm in which water repeatedly pictures God:

> **You visit the earth and water it, You greatly enrich it; the river of God is full of water; You provide their grain, for so You have prepared it.** (Psalm 65:9)

Throughout the Old Testament water is a picture of God, so that when we come to the New Testament it is not surprising to hear the Lord

Jesus cry on that last day of the feast, "If anyone thirsts, let him come to Me and drink" (John 7:37), for water is a picture of God.

Water is also a picture of the Trinity, for water exists in three forms, in three states. It exists in flowing water, it exists in ice, and it exists in steam. They are the same substance, but they are absolutely three different things.

Ice, I would suggest, reminds us of God the Father—stability, immutability. Steam reminds us of the Holy Spirit—the power of God. Water reminds us of the Lord Jesus Christ—the Water of Life today.

Light Is a Trinity

For our final illustration, let us consider light. We are told that God *dwells* in light and that He *is* light. "In Him is no darkness at all" (1 John 1:5). One of the glorious prospects of our future eternal home is that there will be no night there.

Light is probably the most expressive and adequate illustration we have of the Trinity. God is light; God is holy. It is the attribute of the Father, but Christ also is the Light of the World. He declared this attribute when a great sinner was brought to Him, "I am the light of the world" (John 8:12). He was manifest. He is the "light" in John 1:5: "And the light shines in the darkness, and the darkness did not comprehend it."

The Holy Spirit is called light. That lampstand

back in the tabernacle and then the temple bore lights that spoke of the Holy Spirit of God. Zechariah was given a vision of the lampstand which was supplied with oil directly from the olive trees instead of through a middleman. In case there was any question, God provided the explanation: "'Not by might nor by power, but by My *Spirit*,' says the LORD of hosts" (Zechariah 4:6, emphasis mine).

In the Book of Revelation, John was given the vision of God's throne, which is characterized by light:

> **And from the throne proceeded lightnings, thunderings, and voices. And there were seven lamps of fire were burning before the throne, which are the seven Spirits of God** [the complete Spirit of God—the Holy Spirit]. (4:5)

Light is probably the best picture we have of God. Paul brings all three Persons together under this figure:

> **For it is the God who commanded light to shine out of darkness who has shone in our hearts to give the light of the knowledge of the glory of God in the face of Jesus Christ.** (2 Corinthians 4:6)

Notice that we have been called out of darkness

into His marvelous light. We today are to walk in light. We have made the error of talking about *how* we walk rather than *where* we walk. When a man walks according to the *how*, he always pleases himself, because he can make up his own little rules and say he is spiritual. It is not *how* we walk but *where* we walk that is all-important. Are we walking in the light of the Word of God?

Every ray of light is pure white, and we always associate that white with God. You can pass a ray of light through a prism, which will divide it into three primary colors. These three elementary colors are yellow, red, and blue. Yellow speaks of the holiness of the Father; red speaks of God the Son who shed His blood for you and for me; blue speaks of the Holy Spirit, for blue is the color of truth, and He is the Spirit of truth. You can push the yellow, red, and blue lights back through the prism and get one white light—three in one.

I am told that the flowers we see do not have any color whatsoever, that actually they and everything else are colorless. I look at these multicolored flowers and am told that although they are colorless, they have the power to absorb or reject the light rays falling upon them. For example, the yellow daffodil absorbs all the color rays except yellow, and since it rejects yellow, I see it as a yellow daffodil! I don't understand that at all. And if I cannot understand light, do you expect me to understand the Trinity? Yet this illustration from nature helps me.

Selah

When you look at yourself you see a trinity; when you hear music you hear a trinity; when you drink water you are drinking a trinity; when you are walking in light you are walking in a trinity.

We have been treading on the high places—I recognize that. I do not know if you have gone along with me, but I trust that you have. I hope that somehow or other the Spirit of God has let you stand on the fringe and see something of the blessed Trinity. There is nothing more awe-inspiring and wonderful in the universe. Learning how to get to the moon was a triviality compared to the privilege of learning, even in our limited capacity, something of the magnificence of the Trinity.

The Trinity's Plan for Man

Back in the beginning (when I say *beginning*, I mean before God had created anything) there was no vast universe as we have today, there were no angels, there was no creation at all. God was alone. Now consider this: God was love, yet you cannot have love unless you have an object of love. But there has always been the Trinity and the love they have for themselves. God the Father loves the Son, He is careful to tell us that. The Son loves the Father, He tells us so. The Holy Spirit loves both of them, and because of His love for them He is in the world today—this sin-stained world—carrying out their work and His work.

Back in eternity when the Trinity was alone, this great plan by which God is working today opened up for Him as the best plan. We know now that it meant He was to have a creature called man and that this little man would lift his fist in rebellion against his holy God. And his holy God must strike him down. A holy God would be just and righteous to breathe this little world out of existence. And, friends, He would not miss it, for He has other universes bigger and, I think, better than this. Why does He hang on to it? Because in His plan He wants the fellowship of that man down there in sin.

Perhaps at that time the Father said, "I will have to judge that man." The Son said, "Because We love him, I'll go down and die for him." The Father said, "I'll send You." And the Holy Spirit said, "I'll go down afterward, and though I am blasphemed against and insulted, I shall stay in the world with that little miserable man and try to bring him back into a relationship with Us."

This is the reason the Scripture says that Christ was the Lamb slain from the foundation of the world. Friends, the Cross was not an ambulance that God sent to the scene of an accident. The Cross is not God's emergency air-raid shelter that He put up hurriedly to meet a surprise attack. Redemption was in God's great plan at the beginning. According to Galatians 4:4 the Father sent the Son to earth in the fullness of time, and He came forth—born of a woman, made under the law—that He might redeem those who were under the law and that He might redeem you today.

The triune God is involved not only in creation but in your redemption and in my redemption. God the Father loves you; He sent His Son. God the Son loves you; He died for you. And God the Holy Spirit loves you, for He is now at your heart's door knocking, wanting to come into your life.

Our triune God! No, you will not understand Him. He would not be God if you could. But you can bow in adoration and praise and yield that little, stubborn, rebellious heart to your Redeemer, Jesus Christ.

Heavenly Father, we do come to You, thanking You that You have revealed Yourself. And yet, O God, when we consider that which You have revealed concerning Yourself, we find that we are standing on the shore of an infinite sea. We feel like a little child playing in the sand with a bucket and a shovel, a little child who knows nothing of those vast shores and that vast sea. Somehow, by the power of the Holy Spirit, push back the clouds, open our minds and our hearts to receive You, even the Trinity: the Father, the Son, and the Holy Spirit.

We thank You today that You are infinitely concerned about us and that You are engaged in a plan and program to redeem us and bring us to Yourself.

We pray these things in Jesus' name. Amen.

CHAPTER 7

THE TEARS OF GOD

There is nothing so universal and common to mankind as tears. An interesting edition of the *Book of Knowledge*, in describing Homo sapiens, states that man is the only animal born completely helpless. We cannot survive without outside help. The only thing we can do by ourselves is cry. That's all. Probably, therefore, the most natural and human feature of mankind is tears. Giving a memorial address for Henry George, John Altgeld said of him, "He dipped his pen into the tears of the human race."[1] Elizabeth Allen, in writing her lovely poem, "Rock Me to Sleep," has one stanza that goes like this:

Backward, flow backward, O tide of the years!
I am so weary of toil and of tears—
Toil without recompense, tears all in vain—
Take them and give me my childhood again![2]

And Winston Churchill's now famous line, given to Great Britain after the miserable defeat at Dunkirk, "I have nothing to offer but blood, toil, tears, and sweat," reminds us that these things are common to and identify mankind.

But tears are usually associated with weakness and frailty. Unfortunately, they are often attributed to the female of the species. I recall a summer Bible school we conducted many years ago at the church where I was pastoring. My study was located where I could overlook the playground. I had noted at the beginning of school a small boy who brought his little sister. Apparently he had been given instructions to take good care of her because he hovered over her all the time. But one day I heard a little one crying. When I opened the window and looked out, I saw that this little girl had fallen as they ran for the bus, and she had skinned her knees on the asphalt. Believe me, she was letting the world know all about it. As she cried, there was her brother, wiping away her tears and giving her quite a sales talk about not crying. In a disgusted tone he concluded by saying, "Only *girls* cry!" Well, I don't know what he thought she was, but it had an ameliorating effect on the little girl. She stopped crying immediately and ran with him to the bus. Tears, even for that little fellow, were associated with girls!

Women have a reputation for shedding tears. They'll shed them profusely on any occasion—at a wedding and at a funeral, and sometimes they just cry for no apparent reason at all. A perceptive poet wrote:

> Oh! too convincing—dangerously dear.
> In woman's eye the unanswerable tear!
> That weapon of her weakness, she can wield,
> To save, subdue—at once her spear and shield.

But, you know, tears are not only womanly; tears are also manly. In fact, many men famous for their strength have wept. The story is told that Alexander the Great wept when there was no more world to conquer. Xerxes stood on the banks of the Aegean Sea and wept when he saw his great fleet destroyed by the storm. As Napoleon was being taken away in his first exile and the coastline of France that he loved so much disappeared from his view, he stood there and wept. The apostle Paul, a man who was apparently not very emotional, is recorded to have wept. And it is said that Abraham Lincoln, a strong man and a strong president, wept unashamedly during the Civil War when the casualty lists were brought to him. Tears are manly; tears are womanly; tears are human. They're the mark of mankind.

Not only are tears human, tears are also godly. It was a profound revelation for the ancient world—actually for both Jew and Gentile—to learn that there were tears in the eyes of God.

There are two characteristics that the pagan world never ascribes to their deities. Have you ever noticed that none of them ever work? It is beneath a deity to work. Buddha has his legs crossed and is always sitting and patting his fat paunch. That is the picture of all human deities, if you please. It was remarkable when the Lord Jesus could say, "My Father has been working until now, and I have been working" (John 5:17).

The other characteristic is emotion. The gods of the pagans never showed emotion. The Spartans were trained to be like the gods on Olympus, so they were stoic. No young man dared show any emotion whatever if he wanted to be like the gods.

But the Bible tells us that God has shed tears. That's a thought to conjure—our God in tears! Scripture says that God laughs; Scripture also says that God weeps. We have three incidents in the ministry of the Lord Jesus Christ where the Gospel writers inform us that He wept, and those tears reveal the heart of God. It's indeed startling! God in tears? Yes, but these tears are eloquent; as Abraham Cowley put it, "Words that weep, and tears that speak."[3] The tears of the Lord Jesus speak, my beloved, and I want us to look at these three occasions in His ministry when He wept.

Tears of Sympathy

The first incident is illustrated in the briefest verse in the Bible, and I'm confident almost everyone knows it. It is so familiar that it has almost become an anachronism, and we smile at it. But may I say to you that it is a somber verse, a solemn verse, a wonderful verse:

Jesus wept. (John 11:35)

It happened on the way to the grave of Lazarus. The funeral had been conducted several days before Jesus arrived in Bethany, but friends of the family were still there mourning with Lazarus' two sisters, Mary and Martha, who were weeping. We are told that when our Lord came into their presence He wept. Jesus *wept.* Our Lord shed tears; they covered His cheeks, and His body shook with emotion.

He knew that He was going to raise Lazarus from the dead, nevertheless Jesus wept in sympathy—sympathy for those He loved because death had intruded into the family circle. Romans 5:12 states:

Therefore, just as through one man sin entered the world, and death through sin, and thus death spread to all men, because all sinned.

Although death is the bitter fruit of sin, it doesn't mean that God does not sympathize. Jesus' tears reveal how God feels at a funeral. Never has there been a coffin with a lifeless form in it, never has there been an open grave, but that there stands an unseen Mourner who is the Lord Jesus Christ.

We sometimes hear it said that Christians ought not to weep over death. But Scripture tells us that we *are* to weep; it also tells us *how* we are to weep. Paul wrote to the Thessalonians,

> **But I do not want you to be ignorant, brethren, concerning those who have fallen asleep, lest you sorrow as others who have no hope.** (1 Thessalonians 4:13)

We are to weep and we are to sorrow, but not as if we have no hope.

The child of God has a hope that is a blessed hope. We shed tears in view of that hope, knowing that someday we will be reunited with our loved ones. May I say to you that God sympathizes at the time of death. The Lord Jesus took upon Himself human flesh to let you and me know that God sympathizes. He shed genuine tears of sympathy to let us know how God feels. I never have stood at an open casket without that thought in mind.

A deacon of my church in Nashville, Tennessee, was a funeral director. He was a gentle fellow with a very tender heart. He had known me since I was a boy, but after I became pastor he called me one morning and said, "Vernon, I want you to do a favor for me. Last night we went down and picked up the body of a man in a jail. He was a drifter—no one even knows his name. When they picked him up he was drunk, and he died in the night. The body is in my hands now. The county pays for the funeral, and there would be nothing in it for you—but I just don't like to bury a fellow this way. I wonder if you'd come down and have a service? There will be nobody present, but let's bury him the right way."

So I went down that afternoon, went into the little chapel and there was this cheap casket. The funeral director had placed a spray of flowers on top of the casket. Then he came in and sat down, and we had a service. I read the Scripture, had prayer, and made a few remarks—it was the hardest funeral I've ever conducted. You know, there was not a person topside of the earth to shed a tear for him. But I want to say to you, there was standing in the shadows that day, although I didn't see Him, our Lord Jesus who, when He was on this earth, went to a grave and wept. And He was there in the chapel that day, and He wept for that drifter.

God weeps because death is the curse of sin, and when death comes to man it brings tears to the eyes of God. It also means that He will come to you and to me in sympathy in that dark hour. No one else may be able to sympathize; no one else may be able to stand with you. I have found that the most difficult time to minister to anyone is when death has come into the family. But there's one thing sure, the Lord Jesus Christ can and will minister to a heart at a time of suffering, because He sympathizes.

The word *sympathize* is an interesting word, made up of two Greek words: *sun*, a preposition meaning "with"; and *pathos* meaning "to suffer." It means He "suffers with." That's what sympathy is: to suffer with another. It's not to say some nice glib expression or send a little card. Sympathy is when you suffer with another. And I say to you, the tears of Jesus are tears of sympathy.

Tears of Sorrow

The second incident is found in the Gospel of Luke:

Now as He drew near, He saw the city and wept over it. (19:41)

The background is actually the so-called Triumphal Entry. Our Lord had already come into Jerusalem on the Sabbath Day, which was Saturday, when no money changers were there. The record tells us that He looked around and then left. He rejected that temple and that city. But the next day, which was a Sunday, He came into Jerusalem again and cleansed the temple.

Several years ago I traveled to the Middle

East and for the first time approached Jerusalem, not from the west, but from the east. We had flown to the capital of the Hashemite kingdom of Jordan and had gone to the top of Mount Nebo. Having then visited the Dead Sea area, late in the afternoon we drove up to Jerusalem. It's quite a drive through the wilderness of Judea. We came to little Bethany and then made a turn around the Mount of Olives. It was at that moment that Jerusalem first came into view. I must admit, it was a real emotional thrill for me to look down upon that city.

That's where Jesus was when He wept over the city. He had been in Bethany, spent the night there, and then He had come around the hill that Sunday morning. As He did, the city of Jerusalem broke into view. It is said that He then wept over the city. Isn't it interesting that, in the one short-lived hour of His triumph, He wept! The language of Luke here is very strong. Literally, it says He *wailed*! I think if you had been in the neighborhood, you would have heard Him! He took up a lamentation for Jerusalem. He was heartbroken over that city, which was to reject and crucify Him. It's no wonder that they mistook Him for Jeremiah.

Jeremiah was called "the Weeping Prophet." When God chose a man to deliver the harshest message ever given to a city, He didn't choose a brutal, hard-boiled fellow. He chose the man who had a heart as tender as a mother's heart. The message Jeremiah gave broke even his own heart. At one point he turned in his resignation to the Lord because he felt he could no longer take the emotional and physical strain on his body. But he had to come back to Him and say, "Your Word was a burning fire within my bones, and I can't keep silent" (my paraphrase, see Jeremiah 20:9). So he went back and continued to give God's harsh message to His people, shedding tears as he spoke.

When the Lord Jesus wept over Jerusalem, there were some who saw Him and said, "He's Jeremiah!" Well, He was certainly like Jeremiah in that He had a tender heart, but our Lord was not weeping for Himself. Even on the way to Golgotha to be crucified, He could turn and say, "Daughters of Jerusalem, do not weep for Me, but weep for yourselves and for your children" (Luke 23:28). Why was He weeping? Well, He was weeping because of the severity of judgment that was coming on that city. This time His tears were the tears of sorrow—sorrow because of the agonizing suffering those in Jerusalem would experience at the time of their judgment.

We have only to follow history a few years, to A.D. 70, to see why He wept. That is when the heavy tread of the Roman soldiers, under the command of Titus, was heard outside the walls of Jerusalem, and they utterly destroyed that city. An eyewitness, a historian, wrote that no city ever suffered the brutality that Jerusalem suffered, when even mothers saw their little ones taken, a brutal Roman soldier dashing out their brains against the rocks nearby. Men and women died inside that city, and children were eaten by their own starving parents. It was horrible! It was judgment upon a city that had rejected its Savior and King.

No wonder Jesus wept over that city, knowing as He did the judgment that was coming upon them. My friend, Jesus shed His blood to make your salvation possible. He sheds His tears when you reject Him. He was "a Man of sorrows and acquainted with grief. And we hid, as it were, our faces from Him; He was despised, and we did not esteem Him" (Isaiah 53:3). And I say to you, people are still doing that!

This does not mean He is burdened down with grief. The next verse says, "Surely He has borne *our* griefs and carried *our* sorrows" (italics mine). He didn't have any of His own, but He was carrying the sorrows and the griefs of the world upon His heart. He knows today the awful doom of a lost soul. Right now the world would like to forget it, but we can't forget it, my beloved, because the Word of God is explicit here:

The wicked shall be turned into hell, and all the nations that forget God. (Psalm 9:17)

Oh, you can say that's an awful doctrine in this

civilized age! But it's too bad some of these murderers today don't know about it. It might deter our escalating crime rate to know we all have to face up to God Himself at the last. The wicked will be *lost*. God is not a "softy" just because He sheds tears. He weeps because it's not His will that any should perish, but that all might come to a knowledge of the truth.

I want you to notice three verses of Scripture that need to be emphasized in our contemporary culture. They were given to a prophet who spoke to a people who would not listen—very much like the generation we have today. These verses contain two great truths: One is that the wicked are *lost* unless they come to Christ; the second is that it will break God's heart if they do not come to Him. You cannot escape this twofold truth.

God Himself is speaking in the first verse:

"Do I have any pleasure at all that the wicked should die?" says the Lord GOD, "and not that he should turn from his ways and live?" (Ezekiel 18:23)

Can you hear the heart of God there? And then in verse 32 of the same chapter:

"For I have no pleasure in the death of one who dies," says the Lord GOD. "Therefore turn and live!"

There's joy in heaven when one turns to God! There's weeping in heaven when one does not turn. Now notice this:

Say to them: "As I live," says the Lord GOD, "I have no pleasure in the death of the wicked, but that the wicked turn from his way and live. Turn, turn from your evil ways! For why should you die, O house of Israel?" (Ezekiel 33:11)

It was a great grief to the Lord Jesus when His people had to be judged. His were tears of sorrow when He wept over Jerusalem.

And He still sheds tears of sorrow. They are tears of sorrow over men and women who reject Him. He shed His blood to make your salvation possible, and He sheds tears when you reject that salvation. He weeps because it is not His will that any should perish. Oh, how wonderful He is!

Tears of Suffering

Now, the third and last incident is found in Hebrews 5:7:

Who, in the days of His flesh, when He had offered up prayers and supplications, with vehement cries and tears to Him

**who was able to save Him from death, and
was heard because of His godly fear.**

I want you to notice this verse and the context in which it's used. It is actually not at the cross. Rather, it's referring to the prayer our Lord uttered in the Garden of Gethsemane. In this prayer there was not only praying, but there was also crying. It was piercing the night air like the cry of a wounded animal.

The question arises, why did He pray in the garden as He did? Especially, why did He say, "let this cup pass" (Matthew 26:39)? You can find various and sundry explanations of this, and here is where good expositors differ. I suppose there are three popular views. One is that He prayed to be delivered from premature death, fearing that He would not make it to the cross. The second is that He prayed because of fear of death. And the third explanation is that it was because He would be separated from the Father. I do not mean to discount any one of these, and yet I do not think any one, or all three, is adequate.

If you will, notice the verse very carefully again:

**Who, in the days of His flesh, when He
had offered up prayers and supplications,
with vehement cries and tears to Him
who was able to save Him from death, and
was heard because of His godly fear.**

Notice that Jesus was heard. If He prayed to be delivered from death, then that prayer was not answered, because He died; but it says that He *was* heard. The writer is actually saying that Jesus prayed to be saved *out of* death, that is, by resurrection! He's looking beyond His death to resurrection morning! I do not think He had any fear of death whatsoever, because death would not be the victor. That's the very thing Simon Peter said on the Day of Pentecost, that our Lord did not leave His soul in hades and that His body did not see corruption! Later on Paul could say, "O death, where is thy sting? O grave, where is thy victory?" (1 Corinthians 15:55 KJV).

The prayer of our Lord in the garden was answered—He was raised out of death. On that cross He who knew no sin was made sin for us. "It pleased the LORD to bruise Him" (Isaiah 53:10), and He dealt with His beloved Son as He must deal with every sinner who stands before Him on his own merits. Jesus prayed that He might be delivered out of death and all that death means.

Unfortunately, in the present hour most people are not afraid to die—nor have they been. The pagan world actually teaches that it's a fine thing to die. You may remember that during World War II many Japanese pilots committed suicide by diving their planes, loaded with bombs, right into the enemy. Also, some Buddhists burn themselves to death. There are a great many lost people today who seem not to be afraid of death at all. Men and women kill their loved ones and then kill themselves. They're not afraid to die, my beloved. The liberal has told them that God is dead, that there is no afterlife, that death ends it all, and that the grave is the final resting place. Therefore, when life becomes intolerable down here, multitudes of people choose death, thinking it is the end. But, my friend, it's not the end! It's just the beginning!

A man with that mind-set came to my home in Nashville. It was summertime and I was sitting out on the front porch studying when this fellow came up the steps. He was not dressed very well, and he pulled out the rustiest gun I had ever seen—it looked like a .45 to me. He said, "If you don't give me some reason to live, I'm going to kill myself."

Well, I said this to him: "I don't know what your problem is, and I don't even know what to say to you. But I will say this, if you prove to me that death ends it all, I'll go and get you a better gun than the one you've got there and let you do a good job of it."

He put down the gun and asked, "What do you mean?"

I said, "I mean simply this, my friend. You're just going out of the frying pan into the fire. If you think leaving this life means you're solving something, you are solving nothing. In fact, you're complicating your situation. God put you here to make a decision. He gave you a free will, and He asks you to exercise that."

In Romans 3:18 Paul wrote, "There is no fear of God before their eyes." That's true today. These people don't mind dying, and if the grave ends it all then they've been smart. But if the grave does not end it all, they're the biggest fools the world has ever seen.

The death that the Lord Jesus endured was not an ordinary death. It's a mystery that none of us will ever be able to penetrate. On the day of Jesus' crucifixion God placed a mantle of darkness over that cross for three hours, so no one can describe the sufferings of Christ when He was made sin for you and for me. It is as if the Holy Spirit pulled down a veil and said, "This is too horrid; this is too terrible. You cannot look inside." So our feeble attempts to picture it are a travesty. His sufferings on the cross are not described anywhere in the Bible.

Only this can be said: There were tears and there was blood. They are silent but eloquent symbols of how God feels. They are real and they're genuine. His tears were not make-believe tears; His blood was real blood!

Our problem today is that we are afraid to face up to reality. And that's the reason liquor, drug abuse, and even television are so popular. Someone has written that the ostrich-like habit of burying one's thinking in the sands of the past makes for mental comfort. It most certainly does not make for realism, which involves facing and accepting the facts. There are very few who will face up to reality in our day. Years ago in England, Margaret Fuller, a writer with a great mind, stated, "I accept the Universe!" And when someone told Thomas Carlyle what she had said, he replied, "Well, she'd better!"

My friend, you had better accept the facts. You had better deal with reality—not play church nor play at life. A great many people come to church not to be moved but to be entertained. They do not come to be shaken—they are already shaky in their faith.

Someone has said that we proclaim today a "balcony" Christianity—it's aimed at the onlooker, the spectator, the nonparticipator. We traffic in unfelt truth. We handle treasures as if they were trifles. We announce the good news as if it were a rumor. We talk about facts as though they were fiction. We claim an experience and we offer a performance. We erect great, expensive launching pads in the form of new churches, and then a little firecracker is fired from the pulpit instead of a mighty missile empowered by the Holy Spirit.

But I offer you something real: the tears and blood of Christ. Both were shed for you. Blood was for your redemption and tears if you reject Him. There is nothing sentimental about God's tears— they are neither emotional nor effeminate. Oh, if we could only get away from this cheap sentiment. But today there are those who say you've got to shed tears to be saved—tears of repentance.

Repentance is not shedding tears. Repentance (*metanoia* in Greek) means a change of mind. It means to be going one direction, then turning around and going in the opposite direction. If turning to God and away from sin produces tears, well and good, but just be sure, my beloved, that you turn around!

My dad used to tell about a boat on the Mississippi River that had a little bitty boiler and a great big whistle. When that boat was going upstream and the whistle was blown, it stopped moving forward and started drifting with the current. The whistle was too big for the boiler to make any progress. A lot of people today have a little boiler and a big whistle—that is, they will shed tears, but they're not going anywhere. They don't even turn around. They just drift.

If you do shed tears, make sure you have turned to the Lord Jesus Himself. I do believe we need a baptism of genuine emotion in the church. Again, we Americans have been accused of having a movie and TV mind. We go and see some movie and weep tears over it—because she didn't get her man or he didn't get what was coming to him. May I say to you, my beloved, a block of ice is weepy also. We can shed tears in church and still be cold toward God.

Let me share with you a letter I received, because I want you to know that I'm not giving you only my opinion in this message but am speaking for others. This is written by Ralph McGill whom I knew as a young man when I worked as a sportswriter for the newspaper. He became an outstanding writer of the South, and he espoused, of course, civil rights, which brought him into prominence. But in the letter sent to me he talked about the church:

> We, as a church, have failed to communicate effectively the Christian message to the present generation, and this generation needs it so desperately. I say this because I have found that the educated man today is the anxious man. He has a sickening realization of his own insecurities, inadequacies, defenses, and aggressions. He has soberly discovered that all men are not inherently good, just, and honest, nor does right always prevail. He's disturbed because the old standards of conduct and control no longer seem adequate. He's beginning to see that all of our meager remedial efforts have failed to stop the inexorable drift of society.

And then he goes on to say that the message in the pulpit of our churches has been watered down. Dr. Stanley High, who was a very prominent journalist and also a Christian, wrote in *Time* magazine some time ago that he was fed up with the "pink-tea" type of church that has no solid message and no saving ministry.

We need to get involved today. Tears are the badge of Christ's suffering. They are genuine. They speak of His deep pain. They tell of His redemptive death and the blood He shed to redeem you. Those tears He shed when He was here on earth were shed for you and me.

> The Son of God in tears,
> The wondering angels see.
> Be thou astonished, O my soul,
> He shed those tears for thee.
>   (Author unknown)

He died to save us; He sheds tears when we reject Him.

Greater love has no one than this, than to lay down one's life for his friends. (John 15:13)

But God demonstrates His own love toward us, in that while we were still sinners [ungodly, without strength], **Christ died for us.** (Romans 5:8)

You can stand on the sidelines today, unmoved and untouched. You can even keep Him from saving you. But you cannot keep Him from weeping over you.

HE IS THE POTTER

The word which came to Jeremiah from the LORD, saying: "Arise and go down to the potter's house, and there I will cause you to hear My words." Then I went down to the potter's house, and there he was, making something at the wheel. And the vessel that he made of clay was marred in the hand of the potter; so he made it again into another vessel, as it seemed good to the potter to make. Then the word of the LORD came to me, saying: "O house of Israel, can I not do with you as this potter?" says the LORD. "Look, as the clay is in the potter's hand, so are you in My hand, O house of Israel!" (Jeremiah 18:1–6)

One Sunday a potter, who also was one of our radio listeners, came to an evening service and put on a demonstration for my church congregation. He brought in a potter's wheel, which was operated by a foot pedal, and on that wheel he put clay. While I was giving the message, he molded the clay into a vessel. It was a very simple experiment, but I never repeated it. The congregation that evening was so intent on watching the potter that I don't think anyone heard my message!

Many years before this, when I was a seminary student traveling from my home in Tennessee to the seminary in Dallas, Texas, I had to cross the state of Arkansas and always passed by a large pottery plant near Arkadelphia. One day we took time out (several other fellows were traveling with me) to stop and see the pottery being made.

There were two very impressive and striking sights there that I have not forgotten. Behind this plant was the ugliest patch of mud I'd ever seen. It was shapeless and gooey. It looked hopeless to me. But out in front of the plant they had a display room, and in that room were some of the most exquisite vessels I'd ever seen.

We went inside the plant, and we saw many potters at work. There they stood, bent over their wheels, all of which were power-driven. Since they didn't have to use foot pedals, they could give their full attention to working with that helpless, hopeless, ugly, mushy, messy clay. They were intent on transforming it and translating it into objects of art. The only difference between that mass of mud out back and those lovely vessels in the display room were these men, the potters, working over their wheels.

Now it was to such a place that God sent this man Jeremiah. He sent him down to see a sermon. Actually it was a very simple sermon, and it is easy to make identifications in this very wonderful, living parable that Jeremiah gives us. We have no difficulty in identifying the clay; in fact, God does it for us. God is the Potter, and He tells Jeremiah that Israel is the clay. Also, it is very easy to make the application to mankind in general and to each man individually. Man is the clay. If I may be personal, *you* are the clay on the Potter's wheel. Regardless of what else may be said about you today, you are clay on the Potter's wheel—as is every person who ever lived on this earth.

The figure of the potter and clay is carried over to the New Testament. We find Paul in his Epistle to the Romans using the same simile:

Does not the potter have power over the clay, from the same lump to make one vessel for honor and another for dishonor? (Romans 9:21)

Then Paul used the other side of this very wonderful illustration when he wrote to Timothy:

Therefore if anyone cleanses himself from the latter, he will be a vessel for honor, sanctified and useful for the Master, prepared for every good work. (2 Timothy 2:21)

So we see that this analogy is carried all the way through the Word of God.

There is a simplicity about our illustration that may cause us to miss the profundity of the message. The meaning is quite obvious when you first look at it—there is the potter, there is the wheel, and there on the wheel is the clay with which he is working. It seems very self-explanatory. The danger is to make a surface interpretation that will not really touch upon the deep message that is here.

To avoid this, we will look for three things: the principle, the purpose, and the person of the Potter. I have attempted to divide it into two great sections, and they belong together like two sides of a coin. First we shall look at the power of the Potter and the personality of the clay. Then we're going to turn that around.

The Power of the Potter and the Personality of the Clay

"O house of Israel, can I not do with you as this potter?" says the LORD. "Look, as the clay is in the potter's hand, so are you in My hand, O house of Israel!" (Jeremiah 18:6)

The Power of the Potter

Like a giant potter, God took clay and He formed man. God is the great Potter, the Creator.

> Then God said, "Let Us make man in Our image, according to Our likeness; let them have dominion over the fish of the sea, over the birds of the air, and over the cattle, over all the earth and over every creeping thing that creeps on the earth." So God created man in His own image; in the image of God He created him; male and female He created them. (Genesis 1:26–27)

> And the LORD God formed man of the dust of the ground, and breathed into his nostrils the breath of life; and man became a living being. (Genesis 2:7)

After man had sinned God said to Adam in Genesis 3:19: "In the sweat of your face you shall eat bread till you return to the ground, for out of it you were taken; for dust you are, and to dust you shall return."

Now let's go back down to the potter's house and stand with Jeremiah as we watch the potter at work. The potter has a wheel, an old-fashioned one. He works that pedal with his foot to make the wheel turn. As he pedals, his hands are deftly, artistically working with the clay and attempting to form out of it a work of art.

Note, now, the first principle: *God is sovereign.* The potter is absolute. That is, he has power over the clay and that power is unlimited. No clay can stop the potter, nor can it question his right. No clay can resist his will, nor "say him nay," nor alter his plans. The clay cannot speak back to him. Do you remember the delightful little tale we heard in nursery school about the gingerbread boy who talked back? Well, this clay can't talk back.

I recall the whimsical story of a little boy who was playing in the mud down by a brook. He was attempting to make a man. He worked on him and had gotten pretty well along when his mother called him. They were going downtown and he must go along. He wanted to stay, but she insisted that he come. By this time he had finished his mud man except for one arm, but he had to leave. When he was in town with his mother and father, he saw a one-armed man. The little boy eyed him for awhile. Finally he went up to him and said, "Why did you leave before I finished you?"

The clay on the potter's wheel can't get up when it wants to. The clay on the potter's wheel is not able to do anything. It can only yield to the potter's hand.

Nowhere, I repeat, nowhere will you find such a graphic picture of the sovereignty of God as this: man, the clay upon the Potter's wheel, and

God, the Potter. You won't find anything quite like this.

Our contemporary generation resists the idea of His sovereignty because this is the day of the rights of man. We hear a great deal today about freedom, and every group is insisting upon its freedom—freedom to protest, freedom to do what it chooses. Today we permit murderers to plead the Fifth Amendment because we must protect their rights. We permit students to deface their schools and torment their classmates because they must have their rights.

But what about God? Doesn't He have some rights? I say to you that God has incontestable authority. His will is inexorable, it is inflexible, and it will prevail. He has irresistible ability to form and fashion this universe to suit Himself. He can form this little earth on which we live to suit Himself. He can take the nations, which He says are a "drop in a bucket," and do with them as He pleases. And you and I as individuals can be nothing but clay in His hands. He has power to carry through His will and He answers to no one. He has no board of directors; He has no voters to whom He must respond. He is an absolute dictator. He is *God*! He has not been able to see something that you and I see every day—He has never seen His equal. You and I live in a universe that is running to please God, and the rebellion of little man down here on this speck of dust that we live on is a tempest in a teapot! Our little earth, as we see in the pictures taken from the moon, is just a speck in the infinity of space. And, my friend, God rides triumphantly in His own chariot.

You will find that the Word of God has some very definite things to say about this:

You will say to me then, "Why does He still find fault? For who has resisted His will?" But indeed, O man, who are you to reply against God? Will the thing formed say to him who formed it, "Why have you made me like this?" Does not the potter have power over the clay, from the same lump to make one vessel for honor and another for dishonor? (Romans 9:19–21)

It was Johann Bengel who wrote, "The Jews thought that in no case could they be abandoned by God, and in no case could the Gentiles be received by God."[1] And Dr. Lange, the great German expositor, said: "When man goes the length of making to himself a god whom he affects to bind by his own rights, God then puts on His majesty, and appears in all His reality as a free God, before whom man is a mere nothing, like the clay in the hand of the potter. Such was Paul's attitude when acting as God's advocate in his suit with Jewish Pharisaism."[2]

God is absolute!

The Personality of the Clay

Now for a moment let's look at the personality of the clay. I realize someone will say, "You have a mixed metaphor here! You mean to tell me that the clay has personality? Clay is formless, it is shapeless, it is lifeless, it is inept, it is inert, it is incapable, it is a muddy mess." The psalmist wrote, "He remembers that we are dust" (Psalm 103:14). Dr. George Gill used to say in class, "God remembers that we are dust, but man sometimes forgets it and gets stuck on himself. And when dust gets stuck on itself, it's mud." We do sometimes forget this, but God remembers we are dust. I look at the clay on that wheel down at the potter's house. That clay has no wish; it has no rights; it has no inherent ability. It is helpless and it is hopeless.

The Scriptures confirm this. For example, although Paul is writing to the Ephesians, verse 1 of chapter 2 can apply to you and me as well: "And you . . . were dead in trespasses and sins." That's man. Then he amplifies this later on in the same chapter: ". . . having no hope and without God in the world" (Ephesians 2:12). That clay on the potter's wheel is no different. And Paul said to the Romans, "For when we were still without strength, in due time Christ died for the ungodly" (Romans 5:6). This is not a very pretty picture.

Very possibly, right now, you are resisting. I don't blame you. Candidly, if this were all that is here, then I would be doing violence to this living parable of the potter's house! If I were told only of God's sovereignty and the fact that I am hopeless and shapeless clay, I would not only tremble, but I would rebel! I wouldn't like it. And if that were the whole story, I would turn my back on God.

But, my friend, I won't turn my back on God because that is not all. Let's turn the coin over and take a look at the other side.

The Power of the Clay and the Personality of the Potter

This is the other side of the coin:

> **And the vessel that he made of clay was marred in the hand of the potter; so he made it again into another vessel, as it seemed good to the potter to make.** (Jeremiah 18:4)

There is not only a principle here, which is that God is sovereign, but there is also a purpose.

The Power of the Clay

Look now at the power of the clay, that clay on the potter's wheel. This wheel, to borrow Browning's words, is "this dance of plastic circumstance." It is the wheel of circumstance.

I do not believe that life's big decisions are made in a church sanctuary. I believe they are made out in the workaday world—in the office, in the school, in the workshop, at the crossroads of life—that is where the Potter is working with the clay. There is the place He is working with you, my friend.

You and I live in a world that seems to have no purpose nor meaning. Multitudes of people see no purpose in life; they find confusion on every hand. Someone has expressed it in a little jingle:

In a day of illusions and utter confusions,
Upon our delusions we base our conclusions.

How true that is of life today!

Look away, for a moment, from the potter's wheel. Behind him we see shelf upon shelf of works of art. Those objects of beauty were at one time on the potter's wheel as clay—clay that yielded to the potter's hand. Once they all were a shapeless mass of mud. What happened? That lifeless clay was put under the hand of the potter, and as the wheel of circumstance turned, he molded and made it into the vessels that now stand on display.

I outlined the Book of Jeremiah for our *Thru the Bible* radio program while my wife and I were staying in an apartment for a few days in Fort Myers, Florida. Every morning we would eat breakfast in the apartment, I would work for a few hours on Jeremiah, and then we would go

over to one of the islands and hunt for shells. I
discovered something: There are thousands of
varieties of shells. My wife bought a book on
shells, and we identified some of them. I never
dreamed there were so many! Anything God does
He does in profusion.

In my hand I am holding a beautiful little
shell that I picked up on Sanibel Island. I had
been working on the eighteenth chapter of
Jeremiah that morning, and when I found this, it
occurred to me that the Lord was trying to say
something to me. God started with just a little
animal, a tiny mollusk, and around it He formed
this exquisite shell. I thought, *Well, since the
great Architect has spent all that time with a little
shell at the bottom of the ocean, what about man
today?*

Look again at those works of art lining the
shelves behind the potter. Don't speak disparag-
ingly of the clay! I'm sorry for what I said about
it. It has marvelous capacity and resilience. This,
my friend, is what our Potter wants—clay. He
doesn't want steel, He doesn't want oil, and He
doesn't want rock. He wants clay. He wants something that He can put in His hand and mold and
fashion. This is the stuff He is after—clay. God
wants to work with human beings.

Someone may say, "Yes, but here is where that
analogy breaks down. The distance between God
and man is greater than that between the potter

and the clay." I disagree with that. Actually God is nearer to man than the potter is to the clay.

This is what I mean: The clay on the wheel down at the potter's house has no will. I do! That clay cannot cooperate with the potter. I can! I quoted the Genesis account of the creation of man for a purpose—God created man in His own likeness. He took man physically out of the dust of the ground; He made man. Then He breathed into his breathing-places the spirit of life and man became a living soul. The clay has no will, but you and I have free will, and we can exercise it. We can cooperate with the Potter.

Now I want to ask the Potter a question: What is Your purpose in putting me on the potter's wheel? Why do You bear down on me? Why do You keep working with me? Why, Potter, do You do this? I'm not being irreverent, but I am like the little gingerbread boy—I talk back. Why, O Potter, do You do this? What are You after?

Well, I go back to the potter's house. Follow me now very carefully. I do not discover here the purpose for my life, but I learn something more important than that. I learn that the potter has a purpose, which is more important to know. I watch the potter there. He is serious; he means business. He is not *playing* with the clay. This is his *work*. He is giving his time, his talents, his ability to working with the clay. Notice again Jeremiah 18:3–4:

Then I went down to the potter's house,
and there he was, making something at
the wheel. And the vessel that he made of
clay was marred in the hand of the potter;
so he made it again into another vessel, as
it seemed good to the potter to make.

Friend, this is not a cat-and-mouse operation.
This is not the potter's avocation, it is his voca-
tion. This is not his hobby. This is not something
with which he is amusing himself. He knows
what he is doing.

This tells me that God is not playing with us
today. He is not experimenting with us. He has
purpose, and that comforts me. This is the second great principle we see here: *The Potter has a
purpose.*

As an onlooker, I stand with Jeremiah and I
ask, "What's he going to make?" Jeremiah says, "I
don't know. Let's watch him." As we observe, we
cannot tell what the finished piece will look like,
but the potter knows. He has a plan. He knows
what he is doing. The onlooker does not know his
purpose, nor does the clay.

But, friend, someday we will know. When God
puts us on the plastic wheel of circumstance, He
means to accomplish something. He has a purpose.

The psalmist said, "I shall be satisfied when I
awake in Your likeness" (Psalm 17:15). Someday
I'll be like Him! First John 3:2 tells us:

Beloved, now we are children of God; and it has not yet been revealed what we shall be, but we know that when He is revealed, we shall be like Him, for we shall see Him as He is.

That's going to be a fair morning, it's going to be a new day! And God will be vindicated—He was not being cruel when He caused us to suffer. Someday, some glorious day, we'll see that the Potter had a purpose in your life and in mine.

Notice again how Paul wrote to the Ephesians. He began the second chapter with the doleful words I have already quoted: "And you . . . were dead in trespasses and sins" (Ephesians 2:1). And if that is all, then I'm through, too. But there is more: "That in the ages to come He might show the exceeding riches of His grace in His kindness toward us in Christ Jesus" (Ephesians 2:7). In the ages to come we'll be a demonstration. We'll be yonder on display, revealing what the Potter can do with lifeless clay. He gets the glory. It will be wonderful to be a vessel in the Master's hand.

The Personality of the Potter

In conclusion let us consider the personality of the Potter. This is the most important and wonderful thing of all. To do this we must take one final look in the potter's house.

I say to Jeremiah, "The potter is a kindly looking

man." Jeremiah answers, "He is. He doesn't want to hurt the clay. He wants the clay to yield so that he can make something out of it." I gaze into the face of the potter. Oh, how intent he is. How interested he is in the clay.

Oh, what a Potter God is! If I could only see my Potter! But the Scripture says I cannot see God. Philip asked the question, which I certainly would have asked, when he said to Jesus,

> **"Lord, show us the Father, and it is sufficient for us." Jesus said to him, "Have I been with you so long, and yet you have not known Me, Philip? He who has seen Me has seen the Father."** (John 14:8–9)

Let us look at the Potter very carefully now. See the Potter's feet as He is working the pedals, turning, turning that wheel of circumstance. See the hands of the Potter as He deftly, artistically, oh, so intently and delicately, kindly and lovingly works with the clay. I look at Him. Those feet have spike wounds in them. And there are nail prints in those hands.

That's not all.

I turn to Matthew's Gospel and read:

> **Then Judas, His betrayer, seeing that He had been condemned, was remorseful and brought back the thirty pieces of silver to**

the chief priests and elders, saying, "I have sinned by betraying innocent blood." And they said, "What is that to us? You see to it!" Then he threw down the pieces of silver in the temple and departed, and went and hanged himself. But the chief priests took the silver pieces and said, "It is not lawful to put them into the treasury, because they are the price of blood." And they took counsel and bought with them the potter's field, to bury strangers in. Therefore that field has been called the Field of Blood to this day. Then was fulfilled what was spoken by Jeremiah the prophet, saying, "And they took the thirty pieces of silver, the value of Him who was priced, whom they of the children of Israel priced, and gave them for the potter's field, as the LORD directed me." (Matthew 27:3–10)

Two verses, 7 and 8, startle me: "And they took counsel and bought with them the potter's field, to bury strangers in. Therefore that field has been called the Field of Blood to this day." They probably did not know what they were doing when they called it the Field of Blood, but I hope you don't miss it. This Potter is more wonderful than any other potter. He shed His blood that He might go into that field and take those broken pieces and put them again on His potter's wheel to make them into another vessel.

Recently, I talked with a woman who has a broken home and a broken life. Is God through with her? Absolutely not. He is patient and willing to rework the marred clay. Is He through with us when we make a failure of our lives? Oh, no. He is not through with us—that is, if the clay will yield to Him. All that is necessary is the clay yielding to the Potter. He paid the price for the field. It's a field of blood. You may look back on your life and say, "Oh, what a failure! I don't think God could ever use me." My friend, He is working with those broken pieces today, and He will work with you if you'll let Him. He has already paid the price for your redemption. You can't make anything out of yourself for Him, and I can't either, but He can take us and put us on the wheel of circumstance and shape us into a vessel of honor.

We are the clay.

He is the Potter.

NOTES

Chapter Five

1. Arthur Hugh Clough, "With Whom Is No Variableness," in John Bartlett, *Familiar Quotations* (Boston: Little, Brown & Co., 1951), 519.

Chapter Seven

1. John Peter Altgeld, "Memorial Address on Henry George," in John Bartlett, *Familiar Quotations* (Boston: Little, Brown & Co., 1951), 684.

2. Elizabeth Akers Allen, "Rock Me to Sleep," in John Bartlett, *Familiar Quotations* (Boston: Little, Brown & Co., 1951), 595.

3. Abraham Cowley, "The Prophet," in John Bartlett, *Familiar Quotations* (Boston: Little, Brown & Co., 1951), 168.

Chapter Eight

1. Johann A. Bengel, *New Testament Word Studies,* ed. Charlton T. Lewis and Marvin R. Vincent (Grand Rapids: Kregel Publications, 1971).
2. Johann P. Lange, *A Commentary on the Holy Scriptures: Critical, Doctrinal and Homiletical,* ed. Philip Schaff (New York: Charles Scribner, 1865).